CALYPSO RESEARCH

W9-AUW-519

PROPERTY OF
MATTITUCK HIGH SCHOOL
LIBRARY

CALYPSO RESEARCH

The Ocean
World of
Jacques Cousteau
CALYPSO

REF
551.4
COU

81806

The Ocean World of Jacques Cousteau

PROPERTY OF
MATTITUCK HIGH SCHOOL
LIBRARY

Volume 21

CALYPSO

Cousteau   Sivirine

THE DANBURY PRESS

All drawings and diagrams by Alexis Sivirine
Preface by Commandant Cousteau

The Danbury Press
A Division of Grolier Enterprises Inc.

Publisher: Robert B. Clarke

Copyright © 1978 by Jacques-Yves Cousteau
All rights reserved

Schematics and drawings by Alexis Sivirine

Translated from the French by Beverly
Sotolov

Printed in the United States of America

123456789

Library of Congress Card Number: 78-64815
ISBN 0-7172-8122-1

The Birth and Realization of a Dream

1933 . . . I am a young midshipman aboard the training vessel *Jeanne D'Arc* on a hydrological exercise in the Bay of Port Dayot, Vietnam. As I watch the local Vietnamese fisherman who guides our launch dive, I am filled with wonder. At noon, the sea dead calm, the heat stifling, he slips naked into the water without gear or goggles of any kind and disappears without a ripple. He surfaces a minute later with a marvelous fish wriggling in each hand and explains with a mischievous smile: "They nap at this time of day." 1936 . . . Between two sea duties, I am teaching for the EOR* aboard the battleship *Condorcet* in Toulon. One of my students tells me of an uncle of his who goes diving off the French Riviera with Tahitian goggles and fishes for groupers, dorados,

* Translator's note: EOR: Elèves officiers de réserve: French corps of men training to be officers in the Reserve.

4

and leerfish with a bow and arrow. . . .

These two incidents fire my imagination. There beneath the keels of our boats lies a little-known yet penetrable universe teeming with life . . . a wild marine jungle separated from our civilized world only by the surface of the sea, that ever changing boundary that conceals the world below from our eyes and has enveloped her in mystery and legend right up to today.

From that time on, my friends Philippe Tailliez and Frédéric Dumas and I talk of nothing but exploring the sea. We visit the pioneers in the field, Commander de Corlieu and Commander Le Prieur. We try out existing equipment—and make some of our own—goggles, fins, mouthpieces, spears (which we soon abandon), cameras, and oxygen tanks (with which I later have two serious accidents).

War comes and finally the Armistice, during which time Emile Gagnan and I develop the aqualung and I make my first two films, *Par dix-huit mètres de fond* and *Epaves,* awarded a prize at the Cannes Film Festival.

Thanks to these two films, I succeed in convincing the Chief of Staff, Admiral Lemonnier, to commission a new Undersea Research Group in Toulon after the Liberation. Later I became captain of our first underwater-research ship, an ex-German diving tender, the M.V. *Ingénieur Elie Monnier.*

Our programs take us from research in diving physiology to minesweeping, from exploring the Fountain of Vaucluse to the first tests of the bathyscaphe. But as varied as these tasks have been, I have always dreamt of exploring the seas throughout the world . . . and in spite of the sage advice of my elders I decide to attempt the impossible and plunge into the Great Adventure. It is this adventure on board *Calypso* that Alexis Sivirine meticulously retraces in the pages that follow.

J. Y. Cousteau

5

"It is this adventure on board Calypso that Alexis Sivirine meticulously retraces in the pages that follow."

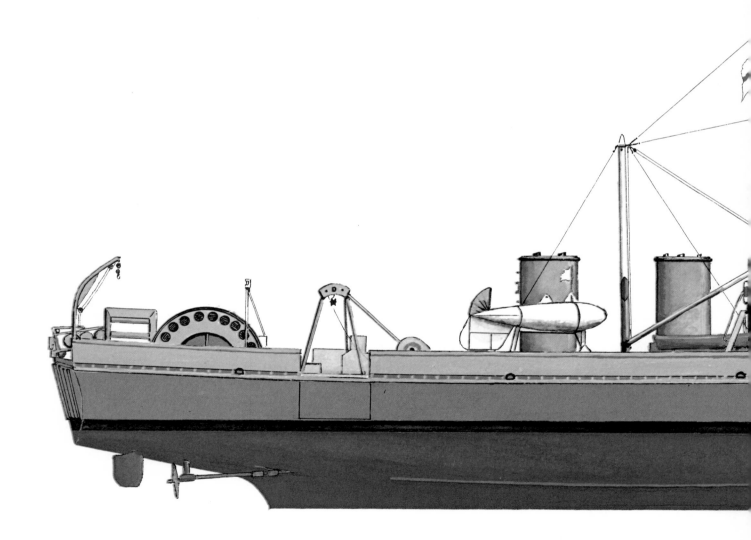

1942—This ship, built in United States, do
only as the minesweeper JB-26. So

ot have a proper name yet. She is known

Great Britain, she travels to Malta.

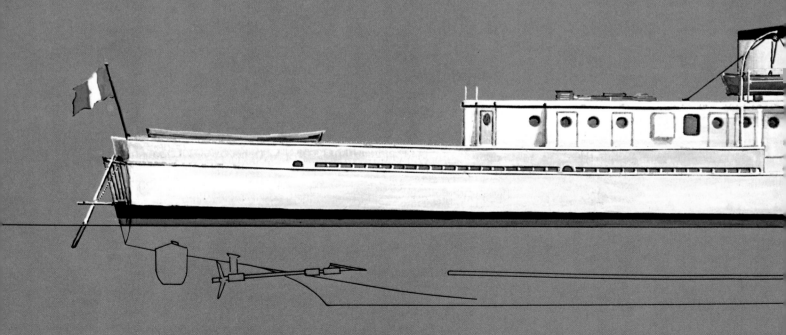

1950—The ship now has a name: she is called Ca

so. Cousteau already shows some interest in her.

1954—Oceanography, research, movies

This is an exciting program for Calypso.

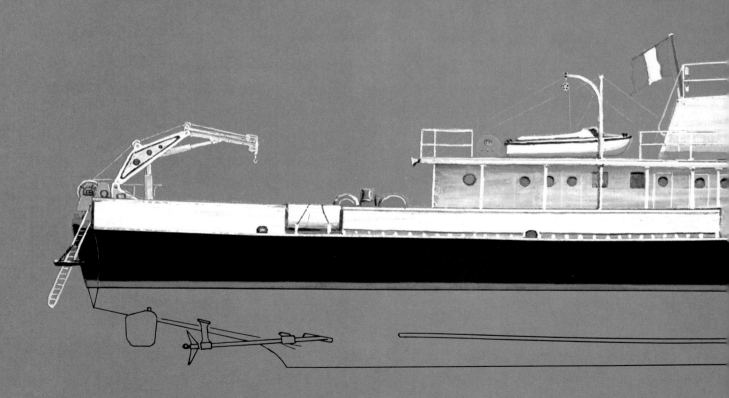

1958—The objective of Calypso does no
follow the evolutio

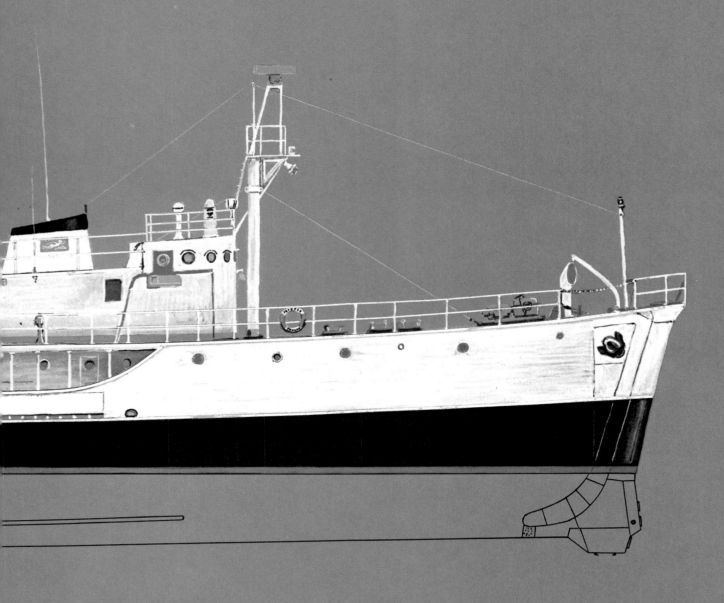

ange, but her shape and the equipment technique.

1959—Carrying a very specif...
to Cartagena r...

dio installation, the ship heads
ncentrate on topography.

1968—With new fittings and even better equipment, Calypso sails to the U.S.A.

Alexis Sivirine has edited the followi

otes from the navigation logs kept on board Calypso.

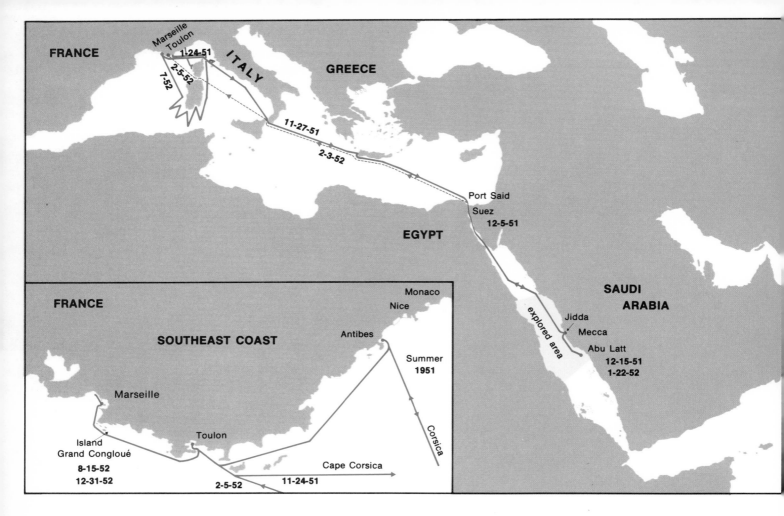

1951–1953

First Encounter with Adventure

A Sailor and a Ship Meet

The *Ingénieur Elie Monnier,* an ex-German diving tender formerly called the *Albatross,* assigned to the Undersea Research Group, provides Jacques-Yves Cousteau with the opportunity to study the equipment necessary for a ship dedicated to undersea exploration.

After Lieutenant Commander Cousteau obtains leave from the navy in 1950 so he can devote his full time to exploring the sea, he sets out to find the right ship. He is lucky enough to meet the head of the naval shipyards in Antibes, André Auniac, who puts him in touch with Noel Guin-

ness, an Englishman with a passion for the sea who offers to buy and outfit a vessel. Accompanied by H. Rambaud, Costeau travels to Malta where he finds an old minesweeper called *Calypso.* The ship's hull is in excellent condition and she has all the qualities he is looking for. The sales contract for *Calypso* is signed in Nice on July 19, 1950, with Joseph Gasan, who has made a special trip from Malta for the occasion.

The ship, which had briefly served as a ferryboat between the islands of Gozo and Malta, is taken to the naval shipyards in Antibes where reconversion is immediately undertaken.

All the deck fittings are redone. The interior accommodations are made more comfortable, special facilities for diving equipment are installed, the radius of action is extended, and navigational aids are added.

All these alterations are very costly. The generous amount of money provided by the sponsor would have been insufficient if Cousteau had not also received donations of most of the equipment and material from various manufacturers and from the navy. Cousteau's dream, shared by an entire community of young scholars, industrialists, and sailors, thus gives birth to what is to become *Calypso*'s mystique.

Calypso thus became a base for marine research and exploration which was totally unique for its time. No such oceanographic vessel for the high seas existed in France.

Calypso's forte during her entire career is in making the new opportunities provided by aqualung diving available to the most diverse scientific disciplines:

—observation of biological population patterns and the behavior of marine animals
—studies of the morphology of coral reefs
—the employment of sensitive instruments by divers
—direct observation of geological structures.

Besides her special equipment, *Calypso* also carries standard instruments, such as corers, grabs, sampling bottles, current meters, and seismic-reflection profilers. These make possible diverse assignments in topography, acoustics, geophysics, physics, chemistry, and geology.

The Great Adventure Is First an Administrative One

After solving the problems of acquiring a ship and obtaining leave from the navy, Cousteau realizes with some uneasiness that running a ship is terribly expensive, and recruiting and maintaining a crew require an administrative structure. He himself wishes to remain free to pursue his projects and his writings. Above all, he wants to establish beyond question the integrity of his ventures.

On the advice of Claude Francis-Boeuf, a young scientist friend, Cousteau establishes a nonprofit organization called COF (French Oceanographic Expeditions). From then on, COF is responsible for commissioning and managing *Calypso,* on condition that a symbolic payment of one franc is made to her owner annually.

Calypso, *displaying British colors, when she served as a ferryboat just before being bought by Cousteau.*

Off the harbor of Antibes, Calypso *is floated for the first time after her reconversion in the naval shipyard.*

First Steps

In June, 1951, the ship is floated and more or less ready to put out to sea. She is far from being completely equipped. But Cousteau, his wife Simone, and Frédéric Dumas, impatient to know how *Calypso* will behave at sea, decide to run the first tests off the coast of Corsica. The crew, improvised by inviting a few friends, is the most extraordinary *Calypso* has ever known. It includes Roger Gary, a manufacturer; his brother-in-law, the Marquis Armand de Turenne; Edmond Mauric, the architect, and his wife; Pierre Malville, a restaurant owner from Antibes; Jacques Ertaud, a young cameraman; a lone sailor from Gary's yacht, nicknamed Malaga; and an engineer by the name of Octave Léandri, the only trained person aboard ship aside from the captain. Léandri, nicknamed "Titi," is the first man hired aboard; he stays with *Calypso* for fifteen years. Cousteau's two sons, Jean-Michel, twelve, and Philippe, ten, are taken on as cabin boys.

There are no lifeboats yet, so Malville lends his dinghy. *Calypso* sails under the French flag, although illegally so, for the papers making her a French vessel are not yet ready. For two weeks she will serve her apprenticeship around Corsica in preparation for her new destiny.

Back from the Red Sea, Calypso on dry dock in Marseille. The observation chamber and the false nose are seen here.

On the bridge, crossing the Red Sea, Captain Saout, Cousteau, and Dumas.

A Close-Knit Team for a Crew

Calypso's first voyage of exploration is planned in Toulon amid a feverish atmosphere difficult to describe. An ambitious, multi-faceted program is organized. Simone and Jacques Cousteau devote a major part of their personal resources to the undertaking. The navy either loans or donates a great deal of equipment. The number of crew members who will receive pay is reduced to the barest minimum, and everyone, including the scientists, is counted on for help with shipboard duties and the watch at sea.

The navy also detaches *Calypso*'s first skipper to her—François Saout, chief boatswain and an expert in long-distance sailboat racing; her chief engineer, René Montupet, a first engineer; and Jean Beltran, a sailor and diver attached to the headquarters of the port of Toulon. A former navy cook, Fernand Hanen, is also hired. Captain Cousteau and Frédéric Dumas will supervise the diving. Stewardship is assumed by Simone Cousteau. During *Calypso*'s twenty-five years of activity, she, of all the crew, spends the most time on the ship, sailing the seas of the world. It is she who contributes the most to maintaining enthusiasm and the spirit of adventure. The camerman is Jacques Ertaud and the underwater photographer is Jean de Wouters d'Oplinter, an engineer and later the inventor of the amphibious camera, Calypso-phot, and the Nikonos. Octave Léandri will help Montupet with the engine.

A doctor is also needed. Jean-Loup Nivelleau de la Brunnière Véron is hired because of his letter of application in which he presented himself as "single, in excellent health, totally immune to seasickness, and grandson of the famous pirate Véron." But during a relaxed evening a month later, he was to admit to Cousteau that the letter was a tissue of lies. "In fact," he said, "I've never sailed, I don't know if I get seasick or not, and my teeth are in very bad shape. Not only am I married, but I am almost a bigamist. As for my ancestor, the pirate Véron, he was captured and hanged on his first trip at sea."

The scientific team that is to study marine biology is made up of Pierre Drach, professor of marine biology at the Sorbonne; Gustave Charbonnier, an assistant at the malacology laboratory, National Museum of Natural History; and Claude Lévy, an assistant at the Roscoff Marine Station. Geology and the morphology of coral reefs will be studied by André Guilcher, a professor of geography at the University of Nancy; Haroun Tazieff, the famous volcanologist; and Valdimir Nesteroff, an assistant at the Sorbonne. Claude Francis-Boeuf and his assistants, Bernard Calamme, deputy director of the La Rochelle Laboratory, and Jacqueline Zang, a chemist at that laboratory, are responsible for hydrology.

Finally, on November 24, 1951, *Calypso* sails from the Toulon arsenal, headed towards the Suez Canal and the Red Sea to study the coral reefs of the Farsan Archipelago. The crew's almost child-like enthusiasm is quickly put to the test. On November 27th, the third day of the crossing, *Calypso* is caught in a violent northeast storm in the South Adriatic. One after the other the two engines fail. In desperation, the crew is about to try to rig a makeshift sea anchor. But it's just a false alarm—the fuel filters had clogged up be-

cause, after two years of inactivity, the tanks could not be cleaned out completely. The voyage continues.

Diving Enters the Service of Science

More than six-thousand dives had inspired Cousteau to a new concept of oceanography. According to him, man's presence in the water is indispensable for arriving at an understanding of a world for which only theoretical or abstract notions have been formulated. "Il faut aller voir"— we must go and see for ourselves. Thus an oceanography which might almost be called militant is born. It will even bring those now gathered aboard *Calypso* in the service of that cause to the point of diving into a sea full of sharks.

The ship's first voyage is dedicated to exploring the magnificent world of coral, studying the abundance of life found there, photographing and filming its multicolored fish. The Red Sea offers exceptional possibilities for such a program not too far from Toulon, and a subsidy from the National Geographic Society in Washington helps defray expenses. The Farsan Bank, south of Jidda, holds a particular attraction for the explorers. Only the outer limits of the reef had been charted, and as for its center, the maps carried only this fascinating note: "unexplored region, studded with reefs separated by deep but non-navigable channels." This is where the divers concentrate their activities. They pitch camp and set up a laboratory on the island of Abu Latt to be used by the geologists, biologists, and hydrog-

At Grand Congloué, getting ready to set the derrick that will hold the huge pipe of the "air lift."

Grand Congloué, near Marseille, is the first major project of underwater archaeology. The diagram shows the air lift, Calypso, and "Port Calypso."

raphers. In the meantime, *Calypso* makes criss-cross soundings of the Red Sea and, for the first time, proves the existence of basins of volcanic origin which contain extraordinary strata of valuable minerals. They are later studied under the name of "hot brines."

This first expedition is a marvelous revelation to the entire group of divers. The scientific team makes highly interesting observations, brings in a rich collection of photographs and discovers many new specimens of flora and fauna. Some of them are named after the ship or members of the crew—*Calypseus, Saouti, Cousteaui.*

Unfortunately the expedition is deeply saddened by the deaths of Claude Francis-Boeuf and Jacqueline Zang, killed in an accident at the Addis Ababa Airport as they were on their way back to Europe.

By the time *Calypso* returns to Toulon on Feb-

ruary 5, 1952, she has indeed proven herself. Now the task is to extend the application of the new diving techniques to other fields.

A New Science—Underwater Archaeology

After some necessary repairs in Toulon, *Calypso* is ready to put out to sea again to devote herself to a new activity: underwater archaeology. In this field, too, we must "go and see for ourselves." Having had the opportunity to dive at many sunken ships off the coasts of Provence and Tunisia (where they had explored the celebrated shipwreck at Madhia), Captain Cousteau and Frédéric Dumas feel that a systematic excavation of a sunken ship from antiquity has much to offer in the way of naval archaeology. They choose a site which the diver Christiannini had mentioned to Dumas. The wreck is located at a depth of 132 feet, 12 miles off Marseille, along the southern coast of the island of Grand Congloué. It is totally arid and ridiculously small, little more than a large, empty rock.

In July, 1952, Calypso leaves Toulon and adopts the Old Port of Marseille as her home base. She shuttles back and forth to Grand Congloué until January 23, 1953, when she returns to Toulon. During those six months, she serves as base for a team which makes dozens of dives daily. She is to carry out the most important excavation of its kind to date.

To free the wreckage of accumulated sediment and debris, the divers use a capricious piece of equipment, a heavy "air lift," a huge pipe rising 150 feet from the bottom, then curving to follow a boom stretching out from the island, spewing tons of material into the sorting basin set up ashore. The pipe would occasionally clog up, escape the divers' hands and writhe uncontrollably in the water. As a rule, each team makes only two dives a day, spending 15 minutes on the bottom each time.

Everyone is greatly interested in the wreck which probably dates back to the third century B.C. People from all walks of life file aboard Calypso. The commander of the military region is taken down on a dive. Albert Falco joins Calypso on September 22 to stay on as a permanent member. Henri Goiran, Raymond Kientzy (nicknamed Canoë), André Laban, and J. P. Servanti make up the main team around Frédéric Dumas.

A Tragic Dive

A spirit of enthusiasm enlivens the group until November 6, 1952, a tragic date in Calypso's history.

As he arrives at Grand Congloué aboard Calypso that day, Cousteau notices that the mooring buoy to which the ship generally ties up has drifted about half a mile as the result of a storm the night before. Jean-Pierre Servanti, a former diver in the navy, checks out the situation. He reaches the bottom and finds that the chain is broken and the anchor lost. Divers search for it all day long but without success. Servanti then proposes to follow the furrow left in the sand by the chain as it drifted. Cousteau agrees, but the deep dive worries him for the echo sounder shows 230 feet.

Servanti descends and his air bubbles are tracked for a while. Then they disappear. Instantly Falco is in the water, followed by Ertaud and Girault, and Falco finds his comrade unconscious on the bottom. He is brought to the surface motionless. After several attempts at resuscitation, he is placed in the recompression chamber while Calypso makes for Marseille at top speed. Despite five hours of treatment aboard Calypso and in the large recompression tank at the Marine Fireman's Station, Servanti cannot be brought back to life.

The team is deeply grieved, but decides to resume diving. Thousands of amphora and Campanian pottery are brought to the surface, inventoried, and classified. They are sent to the Borely Museum in Marseille.

In Vieux Port, the harbor of Marseille, Commandant Cousteau, Professor Benoît, and curious passersby watch amphoras and various objects being brought back on land after 2,200 years of immersion.

Albert Falco, followed by the rest of the crew, carries the amphoras on shore.

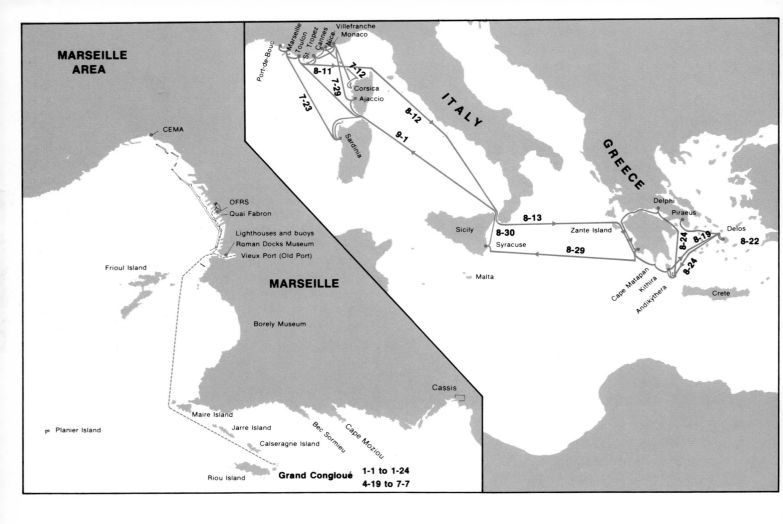

CEMA

OFRS
Quai Fabron

Lighthouses and buoys
Roman Docks Museum
Vieux Port (Old Port)

Frioul Island

MARSEILLE

Borely Museum

Planier Island

Maire Island

Jarre Island

Calseragne Island

Bec Sormieu

Cape Moziou

Cassis

Riou Island

Grand Congloué 1-1 to 1-24
4-19 to 7-7

Port-de-Bouc

Marseille
Toulon
St Tropez
Cannes
Nice

Villefranche
Monaco

8-11
7-12
7-29
7-23

Corsica
Ajaccio

8-12

9-1

Sardinia

ITALY

GREECE

Delphi

Piraeus

Sicily

8-13

8-30

Zante Island

Syracuse

8-29

Delos

8-24
8-19
8-22

8-24

Cape Matapan

Kithira

Andikythera

Crete

Malta

Unable to stay all winter long by Grand Congloué, Calypso departs, leaving some divers ashore.

Port Calypso

Because *Calypso* could not remain moored by the island all winter long without risk, it was decided to set up a hut on the rocks of Grand Congloué, equipped with generator sets, furniture, and various accessories. Thus "Port Calypso" is established. Five or six divers are to live there, regularly supplied with fresh provisions by the *Espadon,* a Sète trawler bought especially for such use. Among them is Raymond Coll, a young man of sixteen who becomes one of the best divers on the team.

Freed of her duties at Grand Congloué, *Calypso* returns to Toulon on January 24, 1953, for a period of much needed servicing.

For both the Red Sea and the Grand Congloué missions, instruments which were nonexistent at the time proved to be necessary. To fill in that gap, Cousteau and a group of Marseille officials decide to establish on March 4, 1953, a second nonprofit organization to conceptualize and develop the prototypes of such equipment. Called the *Office français de recherches sous-marines*—OFRS—this foundation expanded and became in 1968 the Center for Advanced Marine Studies (CEMA).

In April, 1953, *Calypso* returns to Marseille and resumes work at Grand Congloué. Underwater television equipment developed by the OFRS—one of the first such systems in the world—allows archaeologists to follow the work on the bottom while they remain at the surface. A special device makes it possible to televise in very turbid water. In one year, 3,500 dives at a depth of 132 feet were made at the archaeological site at Grand Congloué. More than ten thousand pieces of pottery have enriched the museum's collection. Details of the hull's construction have contributed to our knowledge of shipbuilding in antiquity. But it is not *Calypso*'s role to settle in at a work site near the coast. Her mission is to travel the seas, gathering information and revealing the still little-known terrain, flora, and fauna of their depths.

"Papa Flash"

On July 7, 1953, *Calypso* returns to Toulon and then Antibes. She takes aboard Professor Harold Edgerton of the Massachusetts Institute of Technology, an expert in deep sea photography and inventor of the electronic flash. *Calypso*'s team affectionately christens the newcomer "Papa Flash."

Papa Flash's equipment enables the photographing of animals at great depths that until now could only be examined at the surface after their capture.

In August, 1953, *Calypso* leaves on a voyage of 5,000 nautical miles in the eastern Mediterranean. She will try to find traces of the mysterious owner of the antique ship that sank at Grand Congloué, which had sailed from the Greek island of Delos in the year 209 B.C. The amphoras brought up at Grand Congloué had the letters S.E.S. engraved on their necks, together with dolphins or anchors, probably the marks of a Greek shipowner, Markos Sestios. *Calypso* visits Kithira, Antikýthēra, and Delos, where a villa is identified through its mosaics as the home of Marksos Sestios. She is back in Marseille on September 2d, and again takes part in the work at Grand Congloué.

On September 21st, *Calypso* helps in the rescue of the crew of the Italian ship *Donatello*, which had run aground and broken up on the rocks surrounding the island of Riou in calm but foggy weather.

In November, *Calypso* is back in Marseille. She is equipped with a new radar and a modern precision echo sounder.

Harold Edgerton showing his underwater cameras to Cousteau, Dumas, L. Malle, A. Laban, A. Falco, and Y. Girault.

On arrival in Aden, Calypso, *painted all white, displays the British courtesy flag on starboard.*

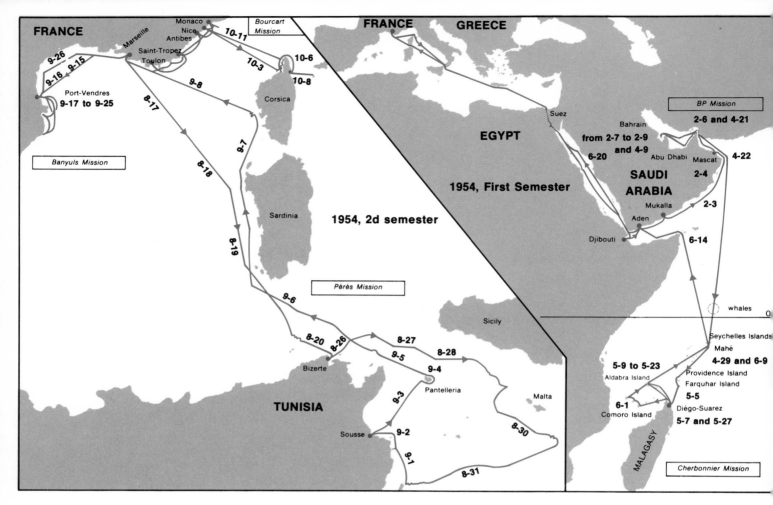

1954–1955

Oil and Films

"Black Gold" beneath the Sea

Calypso sails from Toulon on January 7, 1954. She has been equipped to prospect for oil. The D'Arcy Exploration Company, a subsidiary of British Petroleum, has entrusted Captain Cousteau with a program of prospecting in the Persian Gulf.

Calypso once again steers a familiar course: Port Said, the Suez Canal, the Red Sea. She drops anchor off the Daedulus Reefs. After reconnoitering the coral islands of Yemen, she is caught in a violent storm in the Strait of Bab el Mandeb and is forced to seek refuge in Djibouti. Inspection by divers reveals that the starboard antiroll keel is in very bad shape and the damage must be quickly repaired. The floating dock in Aden is just big enough to accommodate *Calypso* and raise her.

Wallace Brown, a Canadian geophysicist, and Alan Russell, an Australian geologist, embark at Aden. They are to supervise the oil prospecting program.

Calypso stops at Mukalla, puts in at Mascat and then makes a colorful anchorage in Elphinstone Inlet, a narrow bay enclosed by high banks, which has to be the hottest place on earth. The divers undertake a thorough examination of the area of Abu Dhabi, site of the mining concession. Four hundred stations are made; that is, four hundred

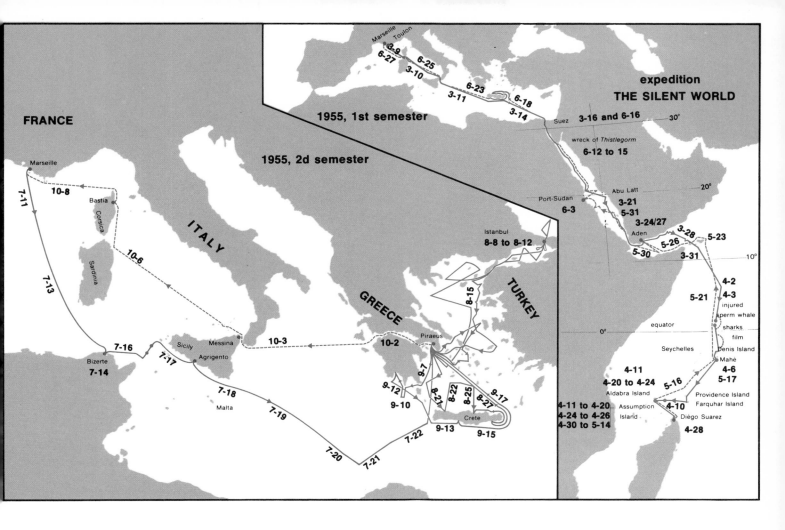

expedition
THE SILENT WORLD

FRANCE

ITALY

GREECE

TURKEY

1955, 1st semester

1955, 2d semester

Marseille
Toulon
3-9
6-27
3-10
6-25
3-11
6-23
6-18
3-14

Suez 3-16 and 6-16 — 30°

wreck of *Thistlegorm*
6-12 to 15

Port-Sudan
6-3

Abu Latt — 20°
3-21
5-31
3-24/27

Aden
3-28
5-23
5-26
5-30
3-31 — 10°

Istanbul
8-8 to 8-12

5-21
4-2
4-3
injured
sperm whale
sharks
film

0°   equator

Seychelles
Denis Island
Mahé
4-6
5-17

Marseille
10-8
7-11

Bastia
Corsica

Sardinia

10-6

10-3

Piraeus

8-15

4-11
4-20 to 4-24
Aldabra Island

5-16

Providence Island
Farquhar Island

4-11 to 4-20
4-24 to 4-26
4-30 to 5-14

Assumption
Island

4-10

Diego Suarez

4-28

7-13

7-16
Bizerte
7-14
7-17
Sicily
Agrigento
Messina

10-2

9-7

9-12
9-10

8-22
8-21 8-25
8-27
9-17

Crete

7-18
7-19
Malta

7-20
7-21
7-22
9-13
9-15

anchorages, often under difficult conditions. It is the season of the khamsin, a raging wind even more violent than the mistral. The accurate location of each station is determined thanks to a Decca radio navigation network installed on nearby islands. A gravimeter is lowered to the bottom to detect anomalies in the earth's gravity due to the presence of oil. The divers take geological samples . . . or at least try to! The bottom is composed of rock so hard that the heavy dropcores cannot penetrate it and the steel pipes come to the surface as pleated as an accordion. The rocks have to be pierced with a pneumatic drill that shakes the divers disagreeably. They descend in an antishark cage but are forced to leave its safety to drill the rock and collect their samples. The sharks circle round the men, but they are not as threatening as the poisonous sea snakes, about seven feet long, that can slither between the bars of the cage.

Aden, Calypso *is raised on a floating dry dock just big enough to accommodate her.*

27

This dangerous and exhausting type of work is making its world debut. It eventually leads to the discovery and exploitation of one of the richest oil sites in the world.

A Million Years Ago: Aldabra

Calypso puts into port in Bahrain and then Doha, on the Qatar Peninsula, to fill up on water and fuel. In Doha we pay a visit to the "Shell Guest," a ship that remained permanently at anchor in the shallow bay to serve as quarters for the technical staff of the Shell Oil Company. For many months, empty bottles of beer were thrown overboard, building around the ship what the crew called the "bottle reef," on which the ship was practically stranded. Good news reaches the ship: the Ministry of National Education has signed an agreement with COF on April 1, 1954, ensuring aid for *Calypso*. It will underwrite a major part of the cost of the expeditions and for several years *Calypso* will act officially as a French oceanographic ship.

Before leaving the Persian Gulf, *Calypso* welcomes new passengers: Gustave Charbonnier, of the National Museum of Natural History in Paris; and James Dugan, an American writer.

Calypso calls at Denis Island and Mahé in the Seychelles. She stops at Providence Island, takes on fresh provisions at Diégo-Suarez and then arrives at the island of Aldabra to study this little known mangrove and coral "sanctuary." Several channels cut through the thick coral ring and lead to the large lagoon where a German cruiser is said to have hidden during World War I. The famous land turtles, found only on Aldabra and, oddly enough, on the Galápagos in the Pacific, wander over the mangrove-covered land. These animals are truly enormous; many must weigh more than 330 pounds. A camp is pitched ashore so that the scientists can study the ground fauna of Aldabra, which includes a unique wingless bird. In the meantime, the divers collect many different marine specimens in the nearby exuberant reefs.

From September 15th to 25th, biological dredgings and samplings are made in the Gulf of Lions with a team of the Arago Laboratory.

For the entire month of October, the geology of the Corsican coasts is studied with Professor Bourcart.

On November 1st, the ship and the crew, both equally tired, return to Toulon for the winter repair period.

The First Diving Saucer

While diving in the outer reefs of the Farsan in the Red Sea, Cousteau found that all the steep cliffs of the reefs stopped at around 148 feet at a kind of beach, believed to correspond to a fossil sea level during a recent glacial period. The beach then sloped gently down to 200 feet, where a brilliantly colored second cliff dropped steeply off into the dark blue of the depths, inaccessible to the divers. Obsessed by a desire to explore the cliffs as far down as a thousand feet, Cousteau begins to muse about a simple device, resistant to pressure and almost as maneuverable as a diver, which would allow him to extend the field of his investigations. Discussing his idea at lunch one day in *Calypso*'s mess, he picks up two soup plates and places the rims one against the other, indicating the shape he wants the device to have. The OFRS goes to work on the idea in Marseille, making a 1/10 scale model of an ellipsoid, 8 inches in diameter and 6 inches high.

In 1955 the scale model undergoes a compression test at the Toulon arsenal with satisfactory results. The device is temporarily called the "Tortoise," in remembrance of the Bushnell sub. But the full-size vehicle, to be completed four years later, will be called the "diving saucer."

On January 27th, *Calypso* sails for Marseille to go into dry dock until the beginning of March. From then on, preparations are underway for the voyage during which the feature-length documentary *The Silent World* will be shot.

The Silent World

Cameras, film, medicine, sundry tools and buoys of all kinds are loaded under the watchful eyes of Frédéric Dumas and Louis Malle, twenty-one, who is to become the famed movie director, and, on March 8th, *Calypso* sails for the Red Sea. She arrives in Port Said on March 14th, but not without first having gone through a violent storm en route! On March 16th, *Calypso* passes through the Suez Canal and then travels down the Red Sea, stopping at the wreck of a ship at Ras Mohammed, easily located by the echo sounder at a depth of 100 feet. The ship's hull had broken open and

Laban and Cousteau are ready to descend in the antishark cage. Rand does the last-minute checking.

To celebrate crossing the equator, "Riquet" Goiran reads a message to King Neptune in front of the other gods.

huge pearl oysters are encrusted on it. Dozens of small groupers trail the divers who find themselves face to face with an incredibly large fish. It so startles Frédéric Dumas and Albert Falco that they pull back and find safety in one of the wreck's narrow passageways. "He was as big as a truck," says Dumas. And Falco adds, "His scales were as big as my hand." The "truck-fish" (as he is then called) is seen again by Louis Malle the next day and later identified as a monstrous wrasse. No record exists of such a common middle-size fish having grown to well over one ton. However incredible, this encounter is a fact.

Reefs and islands give way to one another as *Calypso* sails the Red Sea southward on to the Indian Ocean, towards the Seychelles.

While en route, in the doldrums area, near the equator, in a dead calm sea, the ship comes across an immense pod of sperm whales. Several groups of the huge cetaceans surround *Calypso*. Suddenly a baby sperm whale just 16 feet long, perhaps mistaking the bulk of the ship for its mother, brushes alongside and is caught in the port propeller. The animal is seriously injured and is losing a lot of blood. The divers try to help it but countless sharks have already gathered round and are circling the stricken creature. The anti-shark cage is lowered into the water and the cameramen are soon ready to film the terrifying spectacle. After the first shark attacks, the others rush at the unfortunate infant and tear it to bits. This is the first time such a sight has been captured on film.

The team unwinds from the experience on Mahé in the Seychelles. Then *Calypso* leaves for Aldabra via Farquhar Island, Gambetta Island, and Assumption Island, where giant green turtles are filmed underwater and laying eggs on the beach. The ship stocks up on food, water, and fuel at Diégo-Suarez and then returns to Assumption for two weeks. The island is a genuine paradise for the cameramen! They tame a large grouper christened "Ulysses," which later becomes a famous screen star.

But the monsoon has started to blow. After a second call in the Seychelles, *Calypso* makes her way north in very rough seas, skirts Socotra Island to the north; with better weather, dolphins, porpoises, and whales are filmed near the coast of Somalia. After a call at Aden, she steers a zigzag course through the Red Sea, stopping many times to film the coral reefs and their colorful fish.

Port Sudan is reached on June 3d. By June 12th, *Calypso* is back at her favorite sunken ship at Ras Mohammed, the most beautiful of all the shipwrecks the divers had ever inspected. It provides the cameramen with a long sequence for *The Silent World*. The ship is identified by its bell; she is the *Thistlegorm,* commissioned in Glasgow and sunk during the Second World War by German planes.

After she passes through the Suez Canal, *Calypso* spends a few days off the coast of Crete and puts in at San Nicolò. The team dives with Greek and Turkish sponge fishermen in traditional helmet suits and films them as they work. The "hard-head" sponge fishermen and the aqualungers from *Calypso* get on well together. They share the local retsina aboard ship and sing all night. On June 27th, *Calypso* arrives in Marseille for maintenance after a long journey of 12,000 nautical miles.

The Matapan Trench

For the next four months, with Professor Henri Lacombe, *Calypso* makes hundreds of hydrographic stations in the eastern Mediterranean, measuring the temperature and salinity of the water. A new winch furnished with 16,400 feet of steel cable enables them to lower Edgerton cameras to take pictures at the bottom of the Matapan Trench, almost three miles deep, the deepest trench in the Mediterranean. Many specimens of deep-ocean fauna are collected by means of dredging. Greece, Istanbul, Crete, and Bizerte are visited.

Always anxious to see the men look their best, Simone Cousteau does not hesitate to become a hairdresser.

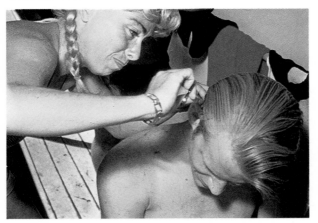

PROPERTY OF
MATTITUCK HIGH SCHOOL
LIBRARY

Anatomy of
the Calypso

1 False nose
2 Observation chamber
3 Observation portholes
4 Sound transmitter
5 Hatchway to false nose
7 Wooden stem
8 Anticorrosion zinc mass
9 Mooring light and folding mast
10 Forepeak and skipper room
11 Chain well
12 Fore windlass
13 Cable guide (crowbar)
17 Windlass electric panel
18 Chef's storeroom
19 Laboratory bench
21 Toilet (head)
22 Wine cellar
24 Forehold panel
25 Hatch hold
28 Cast-iron ballast
30 Movie equipment
31 Bitts
32 Mooring line locker
35 Gas oil tanks
36 Wooden keel
37 Water heater
38 Cameramen's cabin
39 Bridge of light alloy
40 Crow's nest
41 Bow light
42 Cargo spotlight
43 Radar antenna
46 Bell ''JB 26 1942''
47 Cabin
48 Stairway to lower deck
49 Crew cabin
50 Signal station
51 Magnetic compass
52 Gyroscope and alidade repeater
54 1000-watt spotlight with flaps
57 Handwheel shaft
61 Chadburn
62 Remote control for engines
63 Emergency radio unit
64 Radio batteries
79 Second captain and purser cabin
85 Walk-in icebox—8°C. (45°F.)
87 Water tank
88 Radio antenna
89 Radio room
90 Radio transmitters/receivers
98 Captain Cousteau's sitting room
101 Mrs. Cousteau's bunk
106 Engine room annex (the ''Plant'')

115 Refrigerator compressor
116 ''Junkers'' compressor and tanks
117 Air distribution panel
120 Storage engine equipment
126 Life preserver
127 Flag mast
128 Outboard motor room
129 Captain's cabin
131 Oxygen tanks
132 Kitchen
135 Electric stove
137 Mess hall
145 Stern light
146 Exhaust silencer
147 Exhaust pipes
148 Air duct
150 Smokestack fan
151 Diving and technical equipment
153 Main engines
154 Main engine bed plates
155 Oil tanks
161 Starting batteries—auxiliary engines
162 Under-pressure water tanks
168 Telephone booth
169 Main oil tanks
170 Fire engine
171 Propeller shafts
173 Daily gas oil tank
174 Oil drums
178 Hydraulic winch
183 Helicopter pad
186 Diver bags
187 Gas tank for outboard motors
188 Diving tanks
192 Aft hold hatch
195 Diving saucer SP 350 stand
197 ''Duclos'' electric panel
198 ''Yumbo'' electric panel
199 ''Yumbo'' hydraulic unit
200 ''Yumbo'' unit oil tank
201 Ballast for diving saucer
202 Saucer SP 350
203 ''Yumbo'' 4-ton crane
204 Crane hydraulic winch
205 Jack
206 Jib jack
209 Propeller bracket
210 Propeller
211 Rudders
212 Rudder spindles
215 Afterpeak
216 Aft winch electric panel
220 Davit pulley

List of reference marks showing the location of Calypso's quarters and equipment.

1 False nose
2 Observation chamber
3 Observation portholes
4 Sound transmitter
5 Hatchway to false nose
6 Air shaft
7 Wooden stem
9 Mooring light and folding mast
10 Forepeak and shipper room
11 Chain well
12 Fore windlass
13 Cable guide (crowbar)
14 Windlass electric panel
17 Shower room
18 Chef's storeroom
19 Laboratory bench
23 Freezer
24 Forehold panel
25 Hatch hold
26 Extra bunk
28 Cast-iron ballast
31 Bitts
32 Mooring line locker
33 Fore passageway and three cabins
34 Engine gear storage
35 Gas oil tanks
36 Wooden keel
40 Crow's nest
41 Bow light
42 Cargo spotlight
43 Radar antenna
46 Bell "JB 26 1942"
49 Crew cabin
50 Signal station
51 Magnetic compass
52 Gyroscope and alidade repeater
53 Removable NASA antenna
56 Radar screen
57 Handwheel
58 Handwheel shaft
59 "Raytheon" depth finder
69 TV screen
72 Air-conditioning fans
73 Radio and radar generators
81 Cold-water fountain
82 Helicopter pilot cabin and electric gear storage
86 Storage
87 Water tank
93 Photocopying machine
94 "SON" rack
95 "Sonic" ocean depth finder
97 Lockers
98 Captain Cousteau's sitting room
100 Captain Cousteau's cabin
106 Engine room annex (the "Plant")

107 Electric panel
109 25 kwa-380 V transformer
110 25 kwa transformer panel
111 Wheel motor and winch
116 "Junkers" compressor and tanks
130 Four divers' cabin
131 Oxygen tanks
132 Kitchen
133 Kitchen refrigerator
135 Electric stove
137 Mess hall
138 Loudspeaker
143 Davits
144 Smokestack
146 Exhaust silencer
147 Exhaust pipes
150 Smokestack fan
151 Diving and technical equipment
152 Camera battery charger
153 Main engines
154 Main-engine bed plates
155 Oil tanks
160 20 kw CC generator
163 Fresh-water distiller
166 Air compressor for tanks
167 Oil purifier
171 Propeller shafts
172 Daily gas oil tank
173 Main gas oil tanks
175 CO_2 tank
176 "Duclos" hydraulic unit
177 Oil tank hydraulic unit
180 Hydraulic winch control
181 Emergency steering station
182 Mooring line locker
183 Helicopter pad
184 "Hughes" 300 C helicopter
185 Disposable gas tank
192 Aft hold hatch
193 Steel cable drum
194 Lime drums
195 Diving saucer SP 350 stand
196 Engine emergency clutch
208 Folding diving platform
209 Propeller bracket
210 Propellers
211 Rudders
212 Rudder spindles
213 Quadrant
215 Afterpeak
217 Winch motor and reducer
218 Aft winch
221 Aft chain well
222 Emergency anchor

Technical features of Calypso.

The ship's features have changed considerably in the course of various careening. In 1974, *Calypso's* features were the following:

Hulls
Overall length: 139 feet plus stern pulley
Beam: 25 feet
Average load draft: 10 feet
Maximum height above sea level: (radar) 37½ feet
Light displacement: 324 tons
Full load displacement: 402 tons
Full load distance ℓ -a: 30 inches
False nose with 6 observation portholes: 10 feet deep underwater.
Two rudders.

Speed
10 knots with 2 motors running at 900 rpm
7 knots with 1 motor running at 800 rpm

Auxiliary motors
2 GM 6.71 generators
— 6-cylinder motor—140 hp—1,200 rpm
— 60kw, 110 v DC generator
1 GM 2.71 generator
— 2-cylinder motor—40 hp
— 20kw, 110 v DC generator
4 40hp Johnson motors for the barges and Zodiacs

Storage tanks
Gas-oil

4 tanks in afterhold	847 cubic feet
10 ballast tanks	812 cubic feet
Total	1,659 cubic feet

Daily consumption when using a 60kw generator: 950 gallons
Range with 2 days' reserve: 11 days at a rate of 10 knots: 2,640 miles.

For longer trips, Calypso loads 52-gallon tanks on deck:
— 50 tanks or 353 extra cubic feet to go from Dakar to Recife in 1971
— 80 tanks or 565 extra cubic feet to go to Cape Natale in 1968
— 140 tanks or 988 extra cubic feet for the trip to Antarctica and to go from Punta Arena to Puerto Montt in 1973

Oil tanks
2-tank engine—370

gallons + 132 gallons	502 gallons
4 tanks of 53 gallons per engine	212 gallons
Total	714 gallons

4 drums of various oil for the crane, the winch, outboard motors, and for the "Junkers" air compressors
Gas tanks for outboard motors (quarterdeck): 2 disposable tanks of 118 gallons each
Kerosene tanks for helicopter: 6 disposable drums of 53 gallons each

Fresh water

4 aft tanks	1,850 gallons
Ballast tanks	3,170 gallons
Total	5,020 gallons

A distiller can produce 317 extra gallons daily.

Air compressors
2 "Junkers" compressors—4 stages
Power: 30 hp; output 132 g/h; type 4FK115 air at 205 bars; 4 storage tanks 264 gallons each; Feeding ramp for 10 bottles

Propulsion
2 General Motors engines type GMC 8268 A— Straight 8 cylinders
Two-stroke cycle Diesel Engine
Inlet air by lights—exhaust by valves
Pressure-charge: 300 g
Fuel-oil injection pumps
Dry geared engines with separated oil boxes and cooling system
Manual dry gearbox
Positive drive clutch and reverse
Reduction of speed ⅛ in forward position
Capacity 580 hp at 1,250 rpm
Maximum crank-shaft speed 1,250 rpm

"Yumbo" hydraulic crane
Power, 4 tons; equipped with a hydraulic winch; hydraulic generator operated by an electric 40 hp/110v motor; Marrel compressor: 90 bars; in case of emergency can be driven by the winches' generator

Hydraulic winch, including:
2 drums, 1 carrying 9,840 feet of ½-inch steel cable; the other, 3,280 feet of the same cable.
This winch is also equipped with headstocks and a special wheel for nylon cable

"Duclos" hydraluic generator driven by a 40 hp/110v electric motor and a variable flow pump which in turn drives a hydraulic motor and the winches.

Warluzel sounding winch: ⁵⁄₃₂-inch cable

Fore windlass with 3 hp electric motor pulling 2 anchors, 551 lbs. and 661 lbs. and 5 links of chain of 10, or 492 feet each

Aft windlass with 2.5 hp electric motor pulling a 330 lb. anchor and 5 links of chain of 10, or 492 feet.

Electrical equipment: both 60kw, 110v DC generators and the 20kw generator feed many lines, of which:
2 4kwa 220v single-phased transformer
1 25kwa 220/380v 3-phased transformer
1 special radar transformer
1 Allis Chalmers 1,250 w radio transformer
1 voltage regulator for television
1 Special Collins radio transformer

Navigation Equipment
Automatic steering wheel with Hardlandic Brown automatic pilot; can be switched instantly to handwheel.
Brown gyroscopic compass
Ocean Sonic OSR 119T/Raytheon DE 721 A sound transmitter
Radar Decca serial D7 type 808 with 12-in. PPI scope—transmitter maximum power: 75kw

Collins BLU receiver radio
Collins 51 J4 receiver—500 khz to 30 mhz
Emergency LMT transmitter/receiver
Fregate transmitter/receiver
TCS transmitter/receiver—1 600 khz to 4 mhz
100W Collins transmitter—500 khz to 30 mhz—150w telegraph

Sound units
Ampex stereo loud speaker
Marantz amplifiers, 2 × 50 w

Television system
Video circuit with 2 waterproof Grundig cameras and 5 receivers

Fresh-water distribution with hydrophore
Saltwater supply used for cleaning and for firefighting with 2 different pumps

Photo laboratory with darkroom and air-conditioned film storage cabinet

Walk-in iceboxes and many refrigerators

Repair workshop with drills, lathes, grinding wheels, etc.

Recompression chambers to take care of the divers.

2 barges made of light alloy and 4 inflatable boats, Zodiac MKIII; 2 "Bombard" lifeboats big enough to hold 20 people

Beside the permanent features listed above, various pieces of equipment are loaded aboard *Calypso* according to the different missions.
Air lift to remove the mud from underwater wrecks
Underwater gravimeter
Two man diving saucer SP 350
Underwater scooters
SP 500 one man minisub
Galeazzi submersible decompression chamber
Trawler troika equipped with flash to take pictures and films of the sea bottom.
Hugues 300C helicopter with its pad
40- to 50-foot-wide Vulcoon hot air balloons
Decca transmitting equipment
Meteorology data receiver from NASA
Equipment allowing continuous analysis to find out the chorophyl content in the sea water
Apparatus to measure currents
Dredges
Coring devices to collect samples of mud and soil
Water sampling bottles
Rolling measuring device
Thumper sound transmitter to analyze sea bottom
EGG lateral sound transmitter

List of reference marks showing the location of Calypso's quarters and equipment.

1 False nose
2 Observation chamber
3 Observation portholes
4 Sound transmitter
5 Hatchway to false nose
6 Air shaft
7 Wooden stem
8 Anticorrosion zinc mass
9 Mooring light and folding mast
10 Forepeak and skipper room
11 Chain well
12 Fore windlass
13 Cable guide (crowbar)
14 Windlass electric panel
15 Return pulley
16 Anchors
17 Shower room
18 Chef's storeroom
19 Laboratory bench
20 Fan
21 Toilet (head)
22 Wine cellar
23 Freezer
24 Forehold panel
25 Hatch hold
26 Extra bunk
27 Seamanship gear room
28 Cast-iron ballast
29 Fire hose and fire equipment
30 Movie equipment
31 Bitts
32 Mooring line locker
33 Fore passageway and three cabins
34 Engine gear storage
35 Gas oil tanks
36 Wooden keel
37 Water heater
38 Cameramen's cabin
39 Bridge of light alloy
40 Crow's nest
41 Bow light
42 Cargo spotlight
43 Radar antenna
44 Anemometer
45 Hydrography light
46 Bell "JB 26 1942"
47 Cabin
48 Stairway to lower deck
49 Crew cabin
50 Signal station
51 Magnetic compass
52 Gyroscope and alidade repeater
53 Removable NASA antenna
54 1000-watt spotlight with flaps
55 Gyroscopic compass "Brown"
56 Radar screen
57 Handwheel
58 Handwheel shaft
59 "Raytheon" depth finder

60 Flag cabinet
61 Chadburn
62 Remote control for engines
63 Emergency radio unit
64 Radio batteries
65 Shifting porthole
66 Clock
67 Atmospheric pressure recorder
68 Radar console
69 TV screen
70 Automatic pilot
71 Light control panel
72 Air-conditioning fans
73 Radio and radar generators
74 Navigation lights
75 Kerosene tanks
76 Recompression chamber
77 Forward harpoon platform
78 Siren
79 Second captain and purser cabin
80 Chief engineer and chief diver cabin
81 Cold-water fountain
82 Helicopter pilot cabin and electric gear storage
83 Light panel
84 Walk-in icebox +7° C. (45° F.)
85 Walk-in icebox −8° C. (18° F.)
86 Storage
87 Water tank
88 Radio antenna
89 Radio room
90 Radio dial
91 NASA picture receiver
92 Radio transmitters/receivers
93 Photocopy machine
94 "SON" rack
95 "Sonic" ocean depth finder
96 Nikkon photo enlarger
97 Lockers
98 Catain Cousteau's sitting room
99 Captain's bathroom
100 Captain Cousteau's cabin
101 Mrs. Cousteau's bunk
102 "Junkers" air intake compressor
103 Zodiac
104 NASA antenna (1973 position)
105 Floaters
106 Engine room annex (the "Plant")
107 Electric panel
108 4 kwa transformer
109 25 kwa-380 V transformer
110 25 kwa transformer panel
111 Wheel motor and winch
112 Tools
113 Drill
114 Lathe
115 Refrigerator compressor
116 "Junkers" compressor and tanks
117 Air distribution panel
118 Saltwater pump

119 Fresh-water pump
120 Storage engine equipment
121 Return pulleys for wheel rod
122 "Warluzel" hand winch
123 Pulley recorder bracket
124 Veritas marks
125 Antenna VHF
126 Life preserver
127 Flag mast
128 Outboard motor room
129 Captain's cabin
130 Four divers' cabin
131 Oxygen tanks
132 Kitchen
133 Kitchen refrigerator
134 Sink
135 Electric stove
136 Dish cabinet
137 Mess hall
138 Loudspeaker
139 World map
140 General Cambronne portrait
141 Air-conditioned room
      for photo and cinema
142 Barges of light alloy
143 Davits
144 Smokestack
145 Stern light
146 Exhaust silencer
147 Exhaust pipes
148 Engine room hatch
149 Air duct
150 Smokestack fan
151 Diving and technical equipment
152 Camera battery charger
153 Main engines

154 Main-engine bed plates
155 Oil tanks
156 Temperature regulator
157 Saltwater intake
158 Control panel
159 60kw CC Generator
160 20kw CC Generator
161 Starting batteries—auxiliary
      engines
162 Under-pressure water tanks
163 Fresh-water distiller
164 Air tank starter main units
165 Air tank valves
166 Air compressors for tanks
167 Oil purifier
168 Telephone booth
169 Main oil tanks
170 Fire engine
171 Propeller shafts
172 Daily gas oil tank
173 Main gas oil tanks
174 Oil drums
175 CO_2 tank
176 "Duclos" hydraulic unit
177 Oil tank hydraulic unit
178 Hydraulic winch
179 Hydraulic motor
180 Hydraulic winch control
181 Emergency steering station
182 Mooring line locker
183 Helicopter pad
184 "Hugues" 300 C helicopter
185 Disposable gas tank
186 Diver bags
187 Gas tank for outboard motors
188 Diving tanks
189 Aquarium

190 Underwater scooter
191 Underwater electric cables
192 Aft hold hatch
193 Steel cable drum
194 Lime drums
195 Diving Saucer SP 350 stand
196 Engine emergency clutch
197 "Duclos" electric panel
198 "Yumbo" electric panel
199 "Yumbo" hydraulic unit
200 "Yumbo" unit oil tank
201 Ballast for diving saucer
202 Saucer SP 350
203 "Yumbo" 4-ton crane
204 Crane hydraulic winch
205 Jack
206 Jib jack
207 Crane control switches
208 Folding diving platform
209 Propeller bracket
210 Propellers
211 Rudders
212 Rudder spindles
213 Quadrant
214 Afterpeak hatch
215 Afterpeak
216 Aft winch electric panel
217 Winch motor and reducer
218 Aft winch
219 Winch control panel
220 Davit pulley
221 Aft chain well
222 Emergency anchor
223 Stabilizer keel
224 Captain Cousteau's
      personal flag

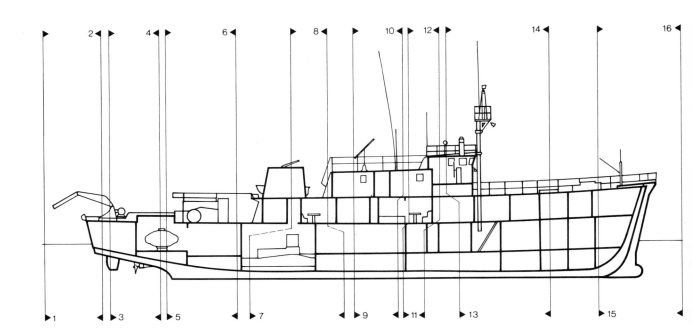

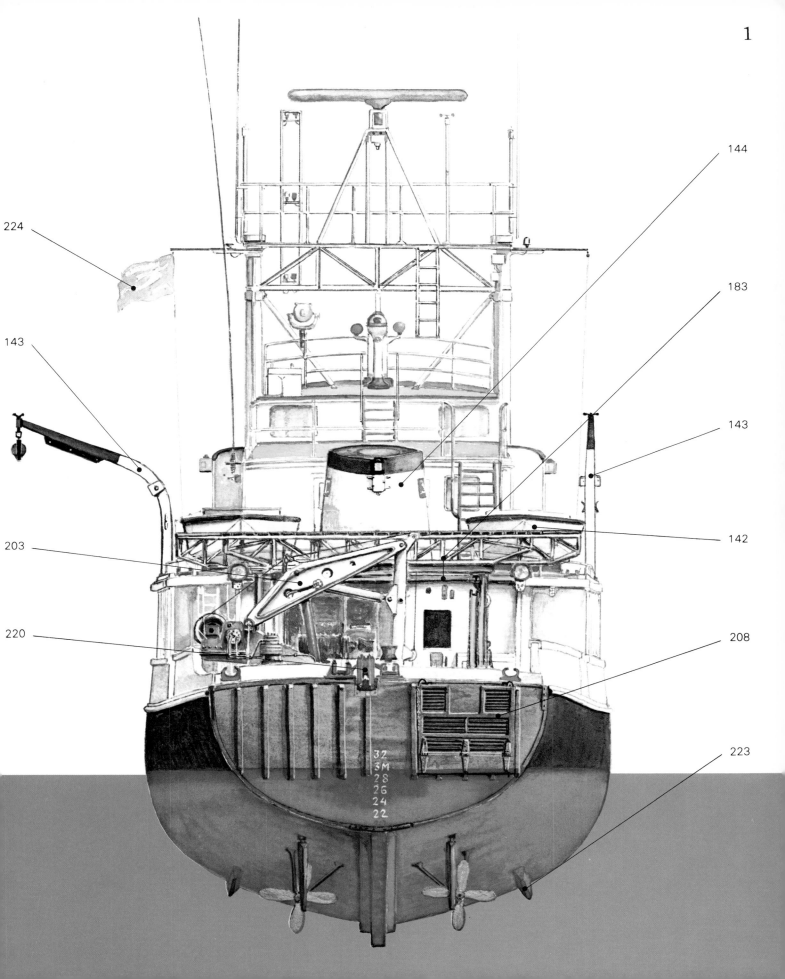

224

144

183

143

143

142

203

220

208

223

204

220

218

219

217

221

20

20

20

21

21

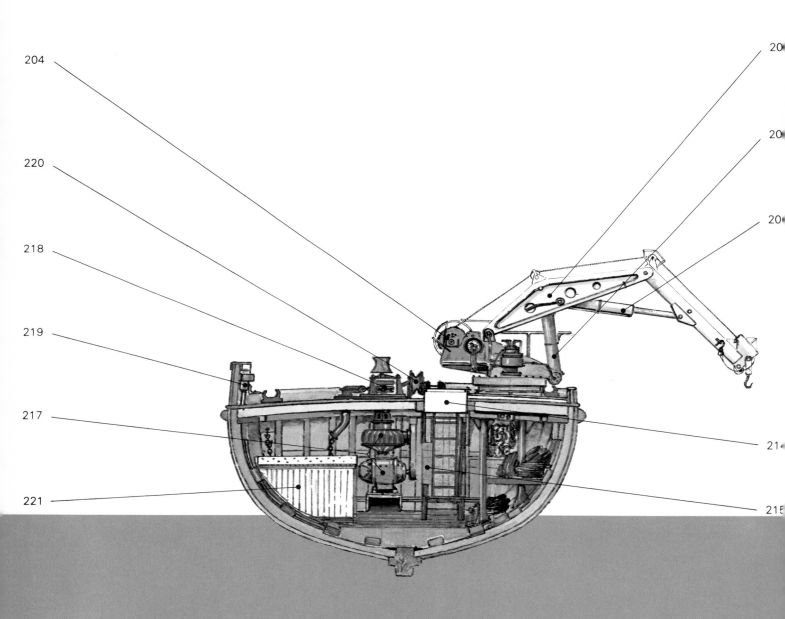

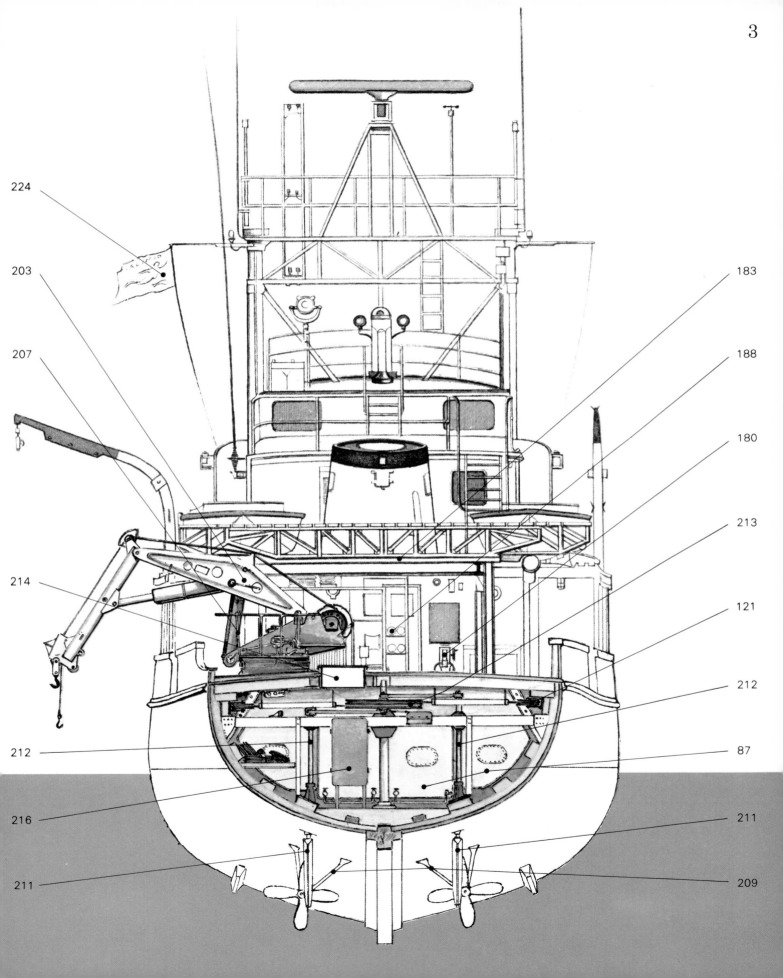

224

203

207

214

212

216

211

183

188

180

213

121

212

87

211

209

4

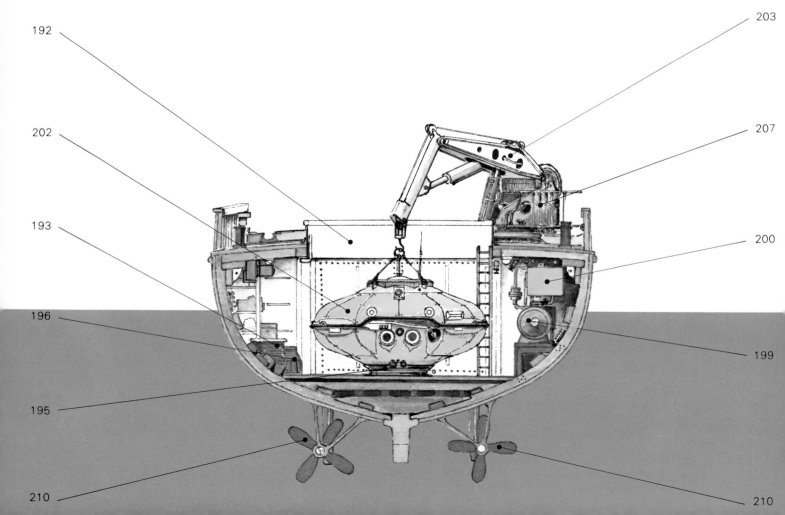

192

203

202

207

193

200

196

199

195

210

210

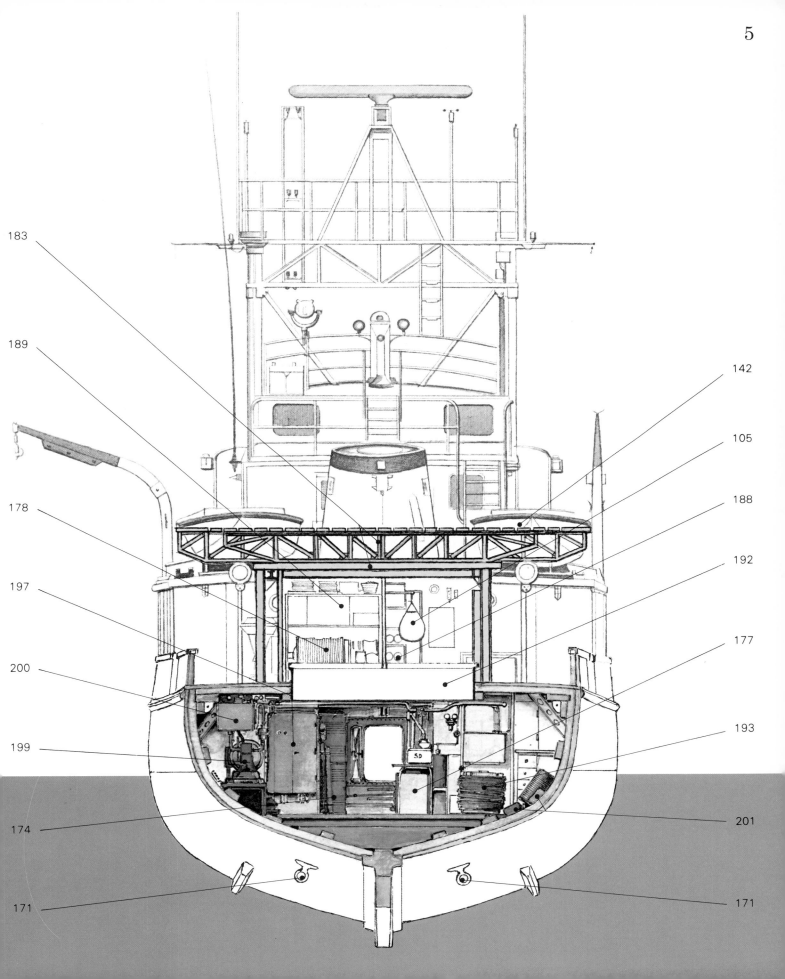

183

189

178

197

200

199

174

171

142

105

188

192

177

193

201

171

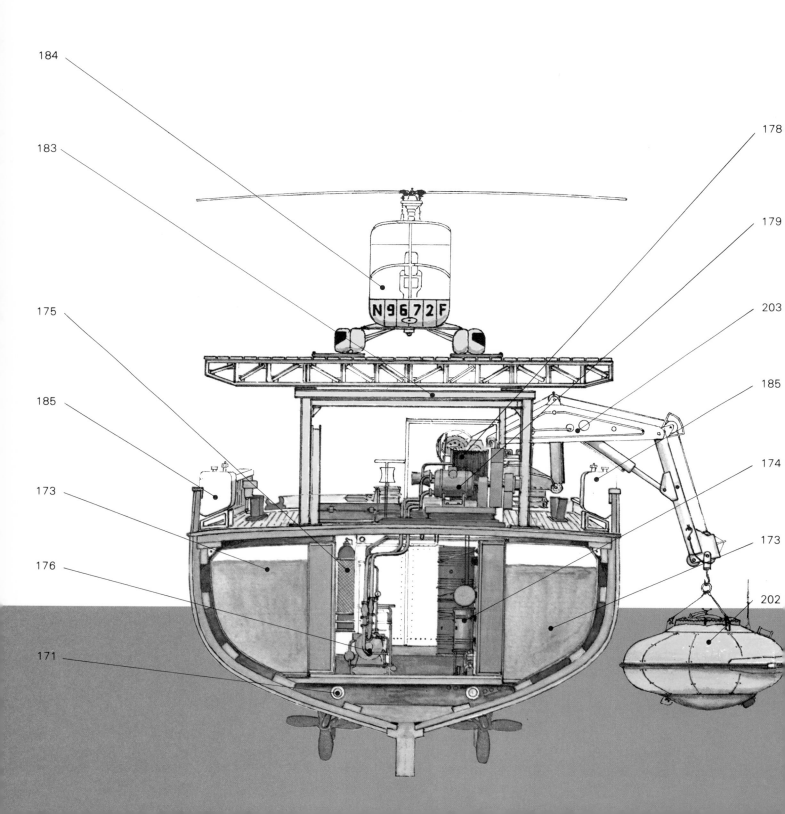

184

183

175

185

173

176

171

178

179

203

185

174

173

202

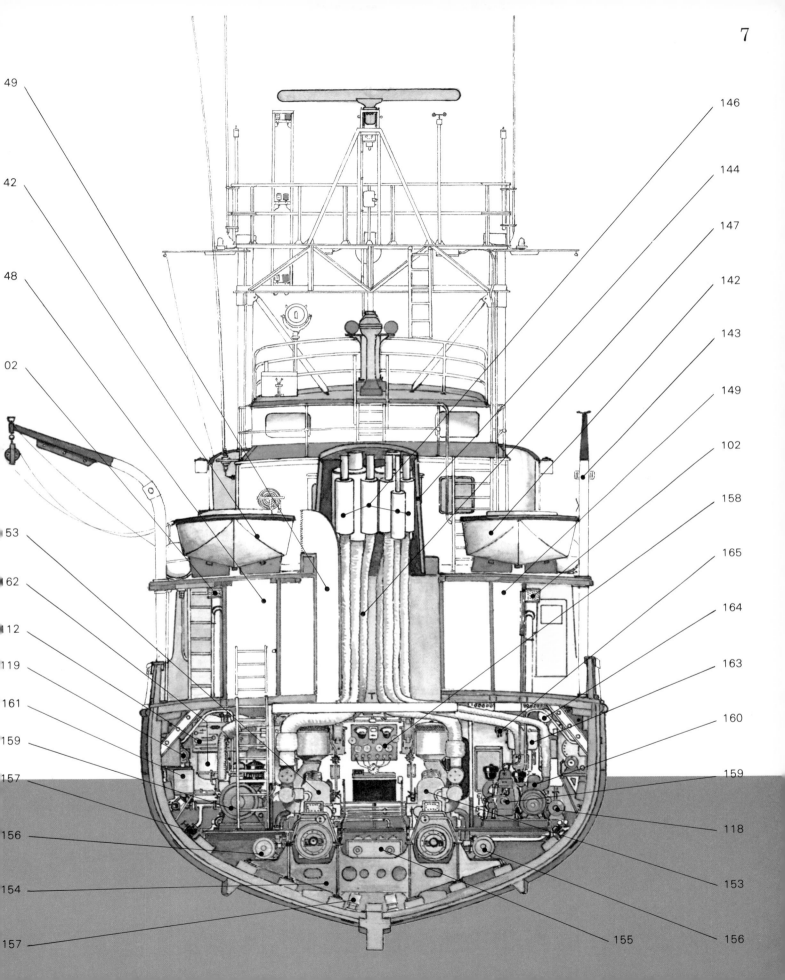

49

42

48

02

53

62

12

119

161

159

157

156

154

157

146

144

147

142

143

149

102

158

165

164

163

160

159

118

153

155

156

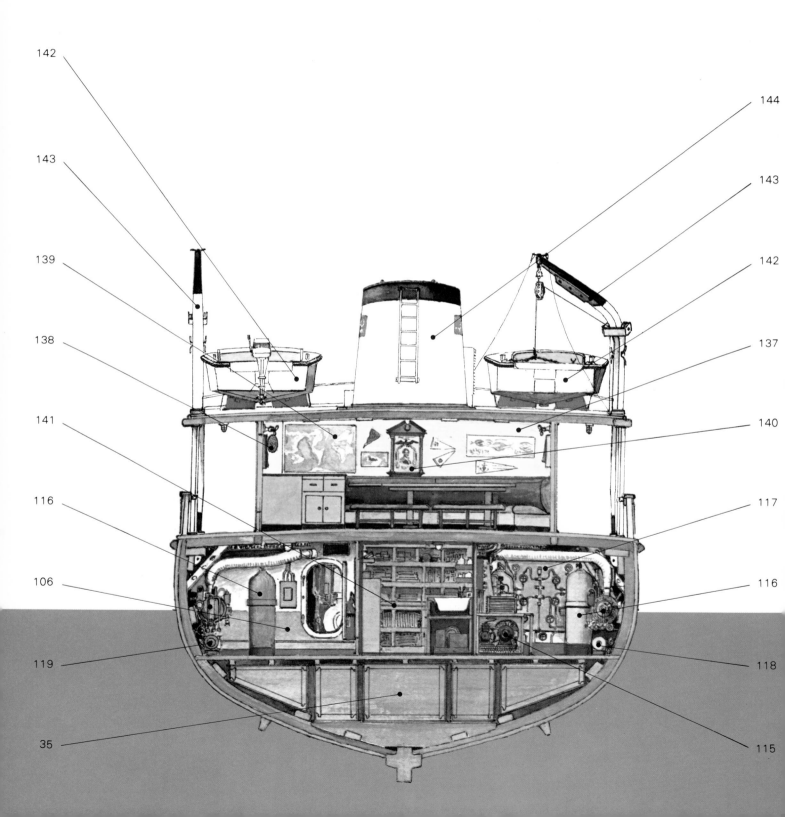

142

144

143

143

139

142

138

137

141

140

116

117

106

116

119

118

35

115

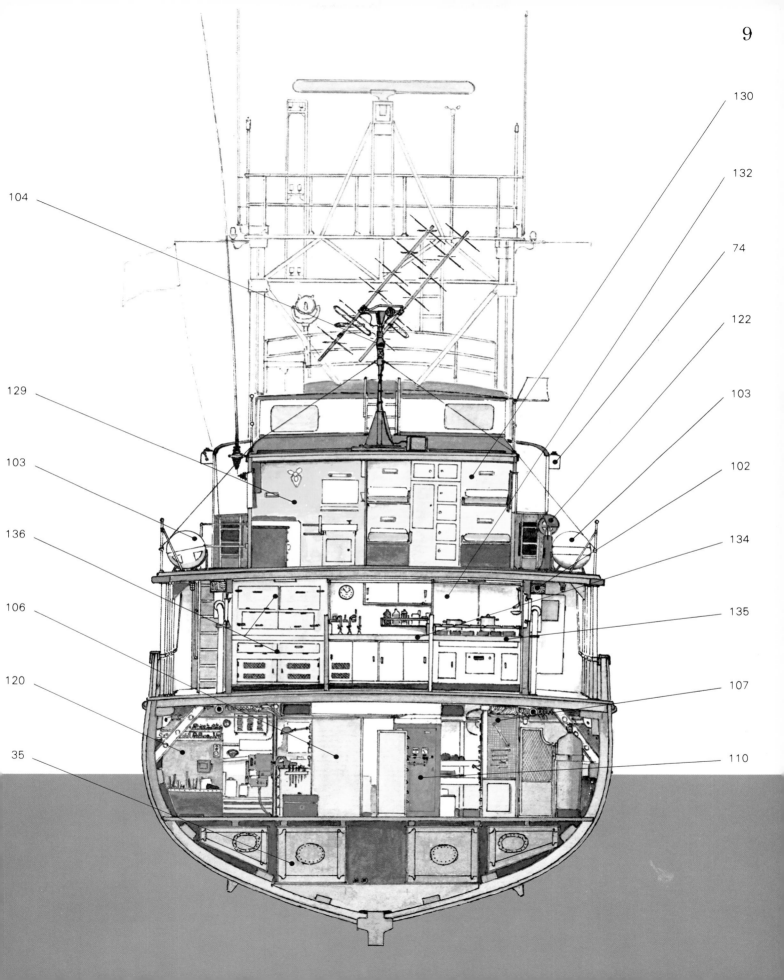

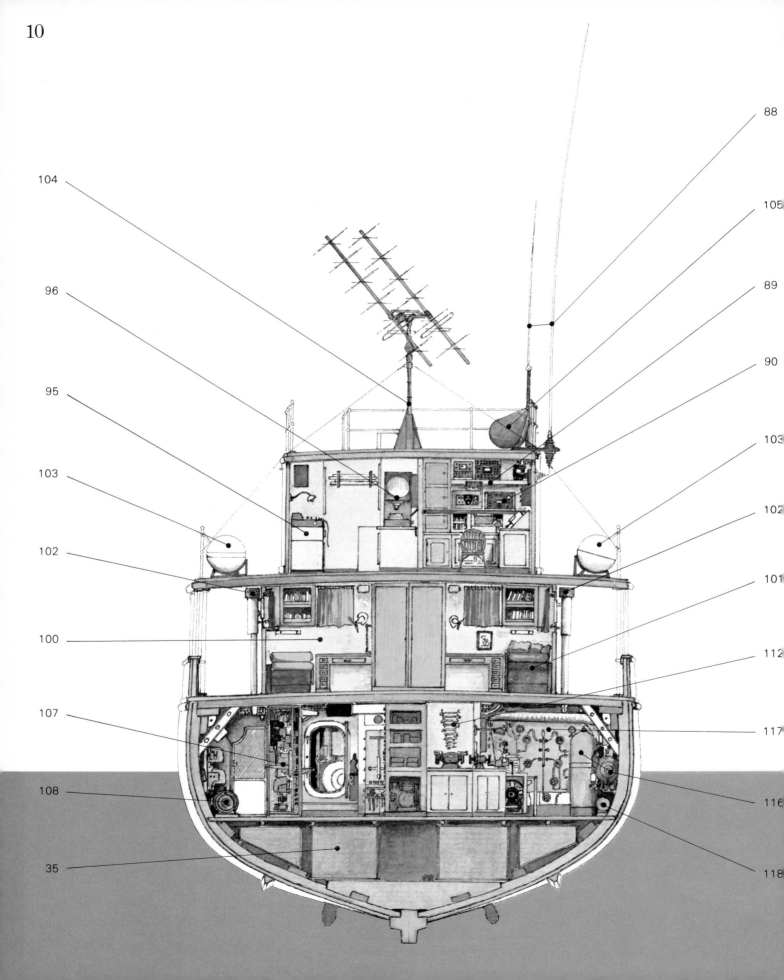

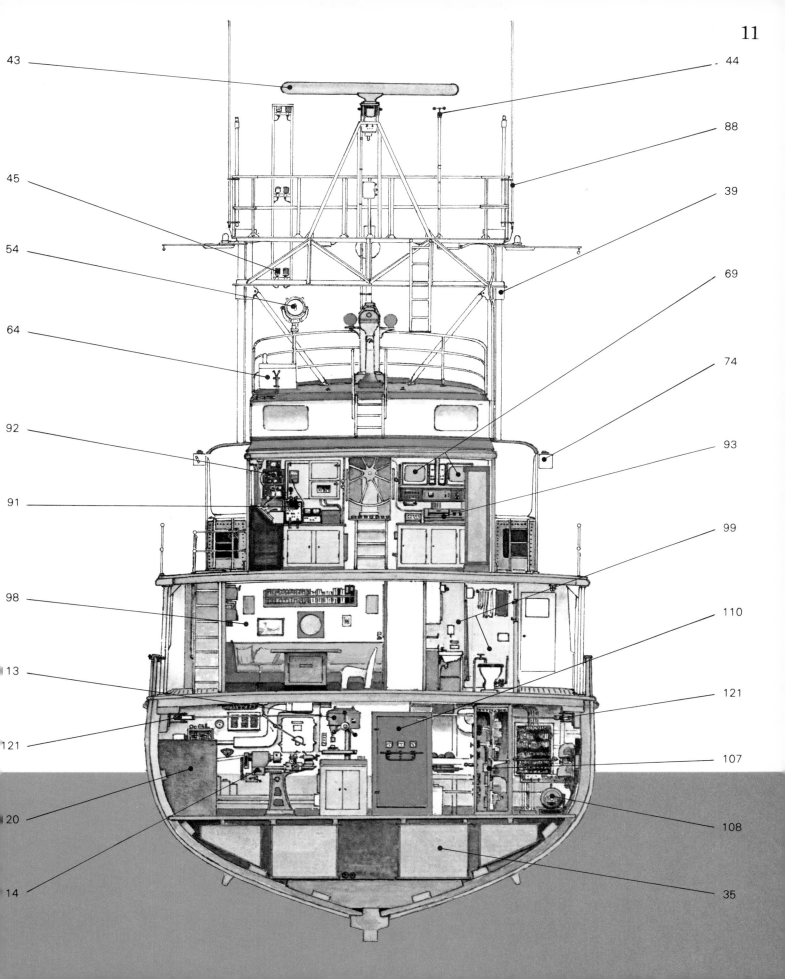

43

44

88

45

39

54

69

64

74

92

93

91

99

98

110

13

121

121

107

20

108

14

35

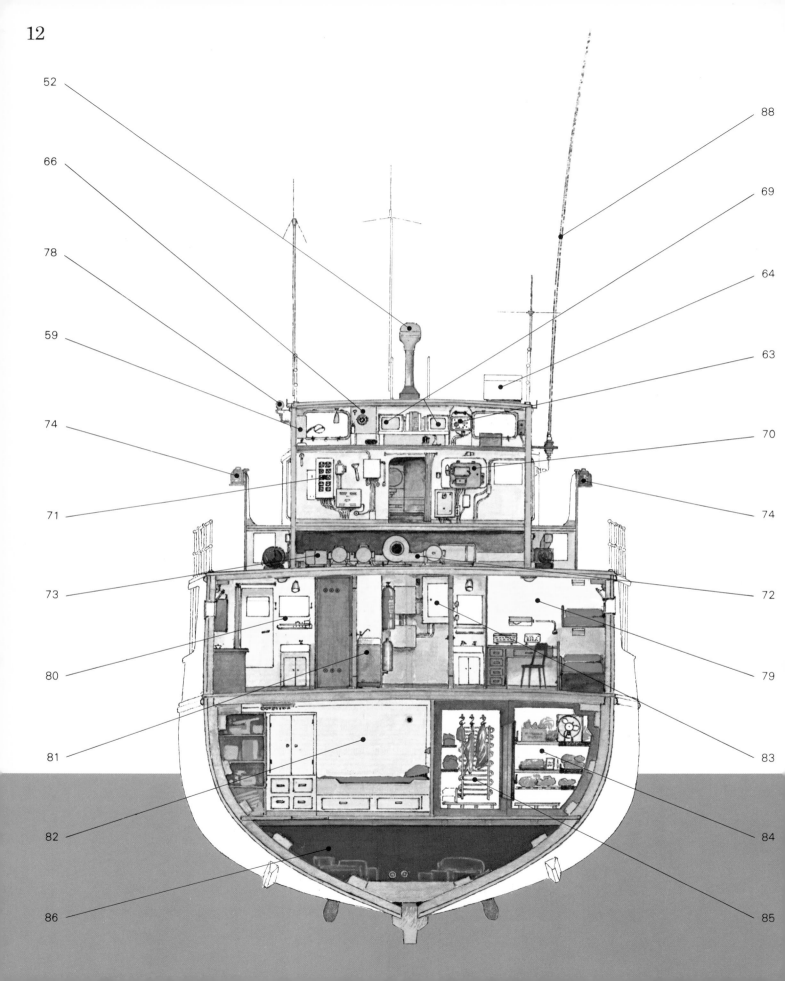

52

88

66

78

69

59

64

74

63

71

70

73

74

80

72

81

79

82

83

86

84

85

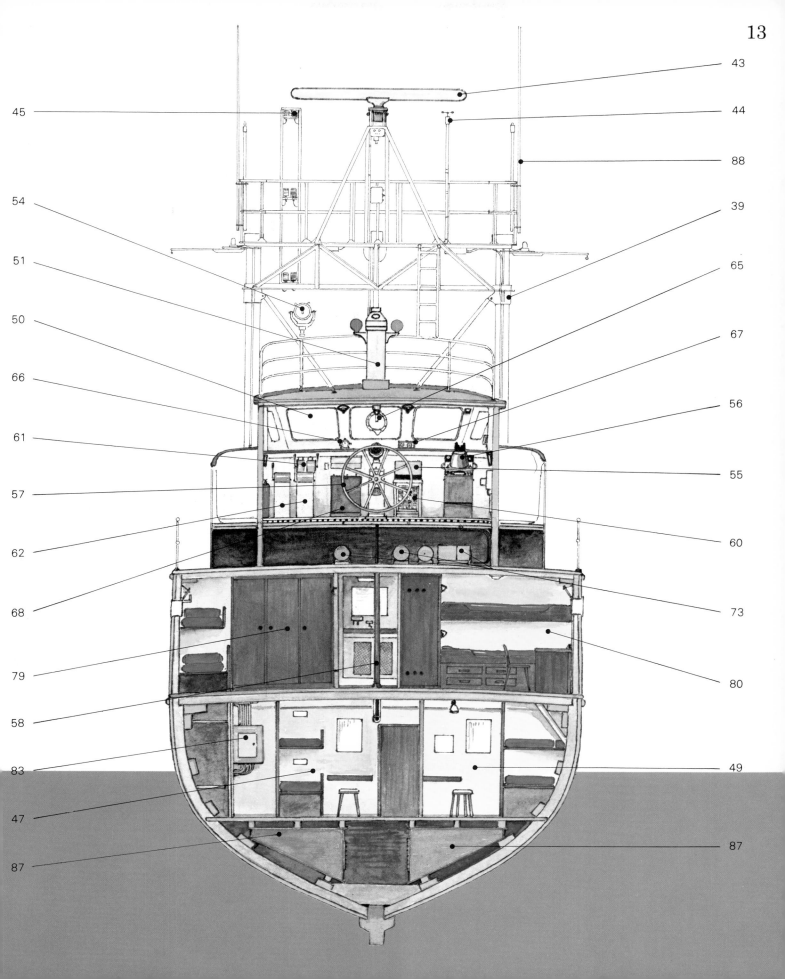

43

44

88

45

54

39

51

65

50

67

66

56

61

55

57

60

62

68

73

79

80

58

49

83

47

87

87

14

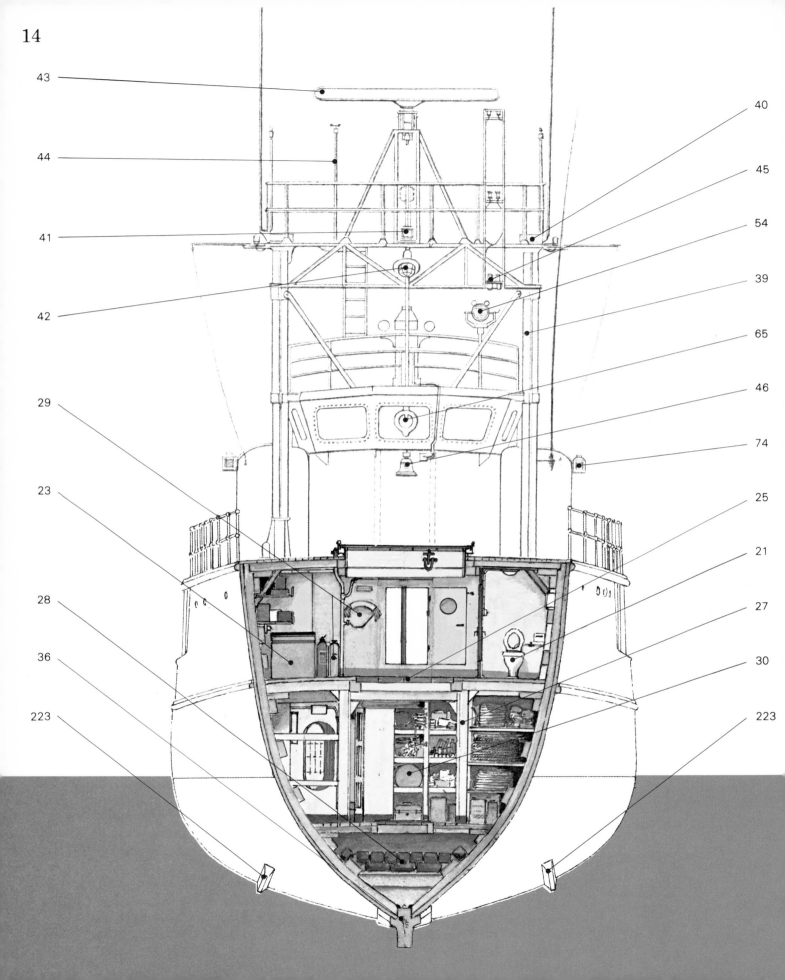

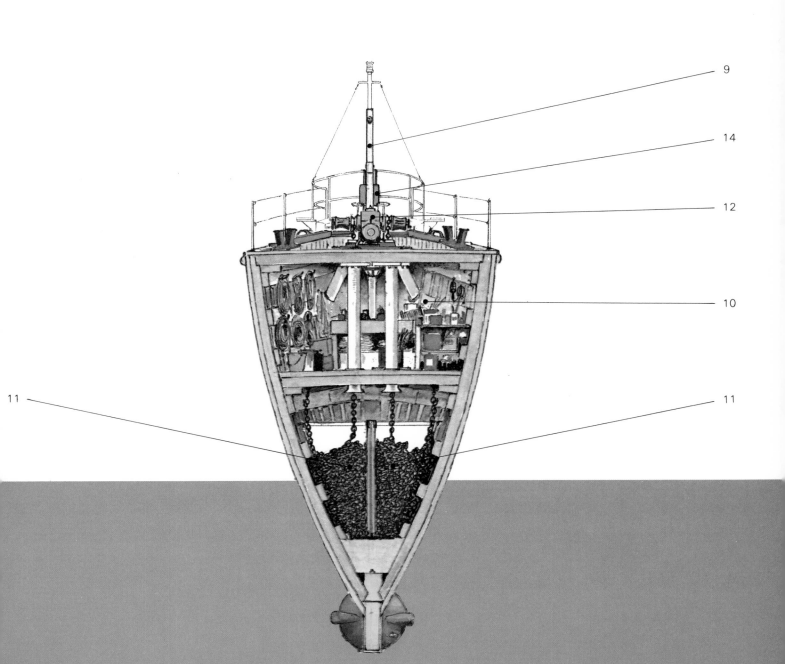

9

14

12

10

11

11

16

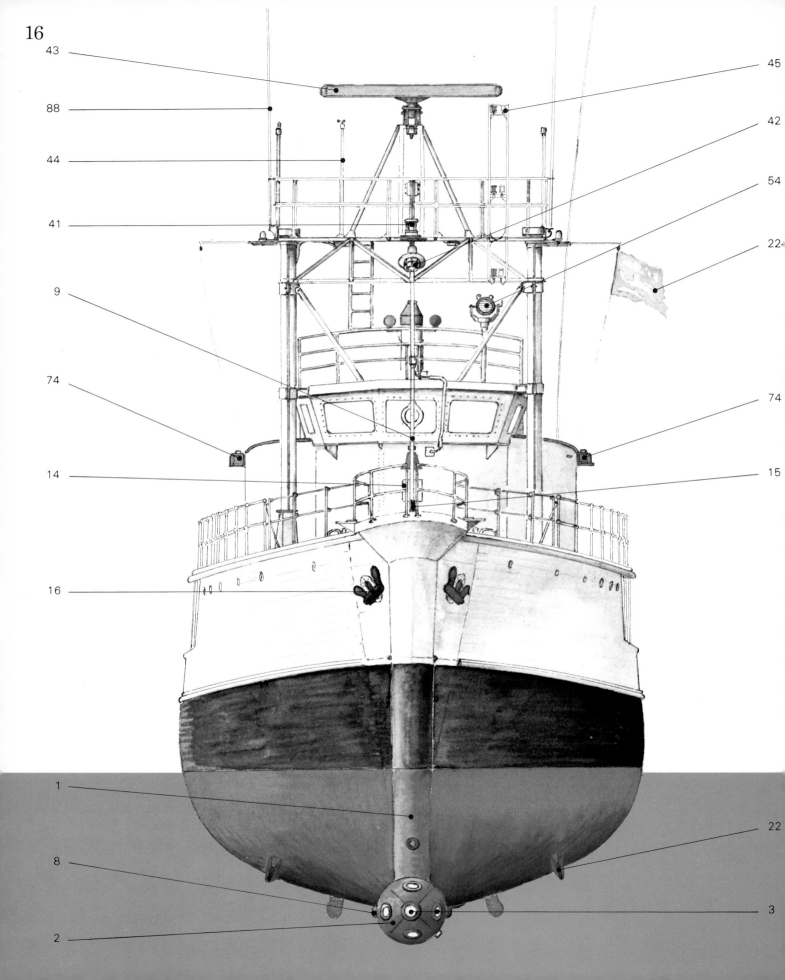

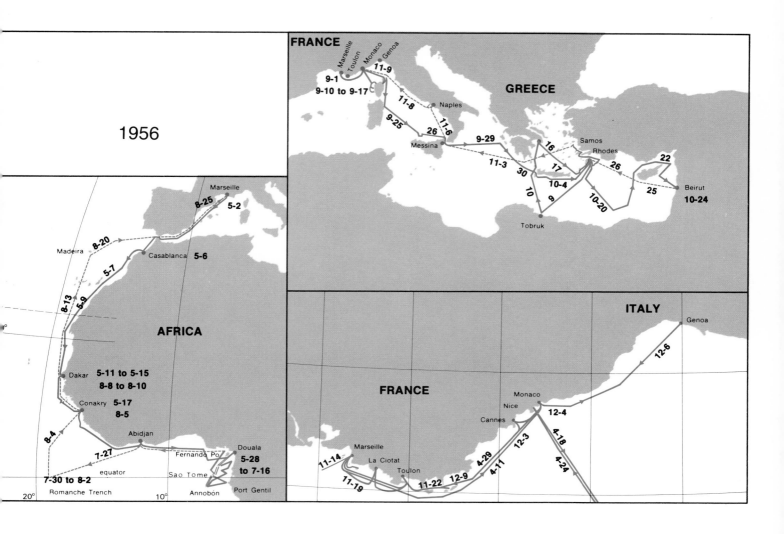

1956

The Deepest Anchorage

During the winter careening at the beginning of 1956, a lot of work is done on the ship, often by the crew itself.

On March 19th, a new electrician boards *Calypso*: Jacques Roux, nicknamed—and nobody knows why—"Gaston."

Calypso devotes herself, under the direction of Professor Bourcart, to taking geological samples with corers and dredges off the coasts of Villefranche, Nice, Ajaccio, Porto, Cargèse and Ile Rousse.

On April 28th, *Calypso* spends two days in Cannes where the film *The Silent World* is shown at the Cannes Film Festival. It is awarded the *Palme D'Or*, the highest award of the festival, and will later give Cousteau his first Oscar.

Calypso *anchors near Príncipe Island, Northeast of São Tomé.*

Towards the "Chocolate Islands"

On May 2nd, *Calypso* takes on a team of scientists at Marseille, led by Jacques Forest of the National Museum of Natural History, and their bulky and precious equipment as well!

The first part of the expedition is devoted to studying the marine environment and fauna off the coasts of Guinea, Cameroon, Senegal, and the Ivory Coast. Special attention is to be given to the Portuguese Islands in the Gulf of Guinea, sometimes called the "Chocolate Islands."

Under the command of Captain François Saout, *Calypso* follows the Spanish coast in rough seas. On May 6th, she arrives in Casablanca.

En route to Dakar, the team fishes for tuna and runs into many colonies of jellyfish. *Calypso* puts into Dakar on May 11th, in rather bad seas.

The schedule drawn up by Forest calls for *Calypso* to work day and night making hundreds of stops at specified points to measure, observe, and collect samples later to be used in connection with various hydrological and biological studies. Nets, dredgers, trawls, bottles, and thermometers are forever swinging overboard. Ports of call give way quickly to one another—Conakry, Abidjan, Douala. From June 2d to July 16th, the activity is centered on the coast between Port-Gentil and Douala, as well as around the Islands of Fernando Po, Principe, São Tomé and Annobón. An epidemic of sleeping sickness spread by the tsetse fly has been raging on Annobón. Portuguese soldiers have been fighting it, after a fashion, by shooting all mammals—dogs, cats, pigs and cows. . . .

Laban rejoins the team in Douala on June 28th. He has with him something as valuable as it is unusual—a special grooved wheel 5 feet in diameter, weighing 440 pounds. The wheel will enable *Calypso* to carry out her next experiment— a revolutionary anchorage at a depth of more than 24,000 feet.

Taming Nylon

On June 25th, Captain Cousteau leaves Abidjan aboard *Calypso*, accompanied by André Laban, his famous "wheel" and Dr. Edgerton. They head for the Romanche Trench in the Atlantic Ocean, situated one-third of the way between Africa and America, where the pioneering experiment is to be run.

Up until 1956, anchorages at depths greater than those permitted by chains were accomplished by an anchor and a steel cable whose weight increased proportionally to the length of the cable. The result was that the breaking point was often reached before the anchor touched the bottom. This inconvenience was partly overcome by the use of special and expensive steel cables of progressive diameter. A nylon line weighs practically nothing in the water and thus retains its strength no matter what length is involved. But nylon also has a fatal drawback—its elasticity. When it is wound under tension, it puts such great pressure on the winch's drum that the drum shatters.

The solution adopted aboard *Calypso* is to haul up the cable by passing it twice only around the famous "wheel," bolted on the axis of the main power winch. The cable is then wound practically without tension on a light separate drum. When all this gear is set up, the quarterdeck is transformed into a spider's web.

Three more days of sailing, while preparations for the anchorage are completed, bring *Calypso* to the equator, 800 nautical miles off the coast of Africa. She is soon in position perpendicular to the Romanche Trench, which is only two or three miles wide, but 24,928 feet deep.

If nylon has the advantage of weighing nothing in the water, this very characteristic also has a serious disadvantage when it comes to maintaining an anchorage. Contrary to the heavy chains which pull horizontally on their anchor when the ship strains, nylon tends to pull towards the upper part of the anchor's shank, thereby causing the anchor to drift. Cousteau finds a solution to the problem in the wooden anchors of antiquity that were linked to their ships by a simple rope made from hemp or jute: although the ancient cables were pulling upward as nylon does, the wooden anchors were heavily ballasted by anchor stocks made of lead. *Calypso's* anchorage is thus made up of a 700 pound anchor, 100 feet of heavy chain, a large pig iron weighing 550 pounds, a steel cable 200 feet long, and finally the small line of braided nylon less than ¼ inch in diameter and 32,800 feet long.

The anchor line is let out slowly on the winch so it does not get tangled on the way down. It takes two and a half hours. The operation is a success the first time around and is the deepest anchorage ever to be accomplished in the world at the time. The echo sounder shows that *Calypso* is not dragging despite a current of one and a half knots. Professor Edgerton takes advantage of the ship's steadiness and has his photographic equipment lowered also on another lighter nylon line. The gear has a flash enabling it to obtain remarkable pictures—valuable evidence of life at great depths.

A detailed map of the bottom is traced by transferring the anchor line to a launch equipped with a radar beacon. In the meantime, *Calypso* makes transverse soundings with reference points carefully marked in relation to the launch. The map proves that the Romanche Trench is part of the famous rift valley of the central Atlantic, the fault area where the forces that give rise to continental drift are manifest. The soundings allow Christian Carpine and André Laban to update their maps and make a plaster mock-up of the trench.

On the second day of the anchorage, a radio message informs the crew of the accidental death in New England of Professor Edgerton's eldest son while testing a new closed-circuit oxygen

Scientists working in the afterroom of Calypso.

diving device. The deep affection of the crew for Papa Flash makes the news all the more tragic. *Calypso* abandons the Romanche Trench, sacrificing the five miles of line that would have taken too long to bring up, and steers a fast course towards Conakry. From there, Cousteau accompanies Papa Flash to the United States. He has the option of rejoining *Calypso* in Madeira.

In order to control the pressure created by the nylon, a flange wheel is installed on the winch and the winding drum where more than 30,000 feet of cable are stored.

After calling at Dakar, *Calypso* sails back to Funchal (Madeira), where extensive testing of the underwater cameras invented by Edgerton is begun again in both deep and shallow waters. *Calypso* returns to Marseille on August 25th.

On September 10th, at 9 P.M., *Calypso* leaves on a program to study the optical qualities of the coastal waters of Corsica under the direction of Professor Yves Le Grand. The penetration of light in deep water, its absorption and diffusion, and the percentage of particles at different depths are measured. The program's itinerary takes *Calypso* to Girolata, Gargalo, Ajaccio, Calvi, Ile Rousse. She returns to Monaco on September 17th.

When Science Clashes with War

On September 21st, *Calypso* leaves on a new hydrology program with Professor Henri Lacombe. She sails from Marseille in a Force 7 wind and is immediately obliged to take refuge in Bastia. Taking advantage of a lull, she leaves for the Ionian Sea where the survey begins in dreadful weather. Off Crete, the clutch of the starboard engine gives way and *Calypso* shelters in a cove to repair the breakdown with whatever is on hand.

Professor Lacombe's program is completed on October 23d. Professor Pérès embarks in Beirut to direct the biological part of the expedition. But scarcely has *Calypso* left port than orders arrive advising Captain Saout to return immediately to Marseille. War has just broken out between Israel and Egypt.

Though he already had strong doubts about the international situation, Professor Pérès is greatly disappointed. He had wanted *Calypso* to sail between the Greek and Turkish islands, but these two countries also were experiencing serious diplomatic tensions. Anastase Christomanos, a Greek citizen and professor on the faculty of medicine at Thessalonika, has to be taken quickly back to Samos. The only thing left for *Calypso* to do is to get home quickly as possible, which she does, meeting many warships in the Aegean on the way.

Calypso is back in Marseille on November 10th. She completes another program off the coast of Genoa and then returns to her home port of Toulon on December 9th.

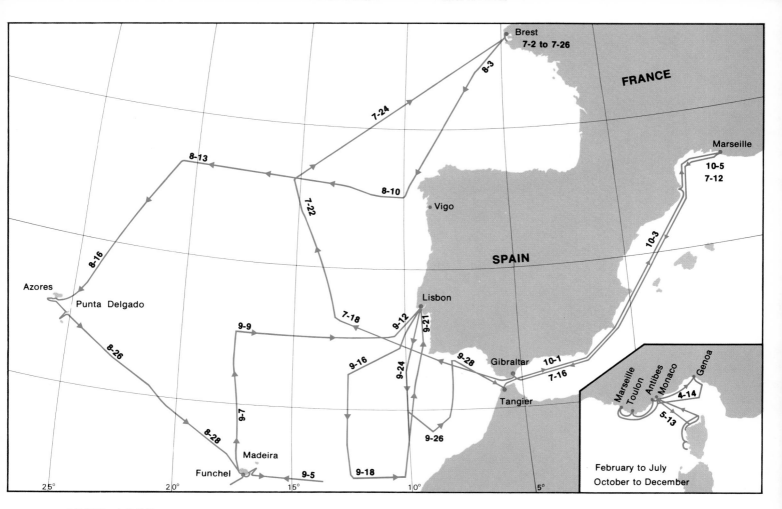

1957–1958

The International Geophysical Year

Calypso Gets a New Look

In February 1957, *Calypso* undergoes in Antibes shipyard several important alterations that Captain Cousteau had decided upon. They are to alter her appearance considerably. The deckhouse, smokestack, and catheads are dismantled, and the spar deck is lengthened. The diving area is redone, the surface of the chart room is tripled, the ventilation for the engines is modified.

On March 30th, *Calypso* leaves Antibes without a smokestack and arrives in Marseille, where a larger hold panel is intalled and a false funnel

constructed. All the instruments are moved into the new chart room, which had seemed spacious enough on paper but is quickly cluttered with a profusion of devices.

A new program awaits *Calypso*. On April 23d she sails for Villefranche where, together with the *Elie Monnier,* she is to accompany the bathyscaphe FNRS III on a series of test dives.

Then Grégoire Trégouboff, director of the zoological laboratory at Villefranche-sur-mer, comes aboard with his buoys, nets, and instruments to study the migrations of plankton.

Another program, directed by Jean-Paul Brouardel, takes *Calypso* to the west coast of Corsica, where sensitive measurements are taken of the

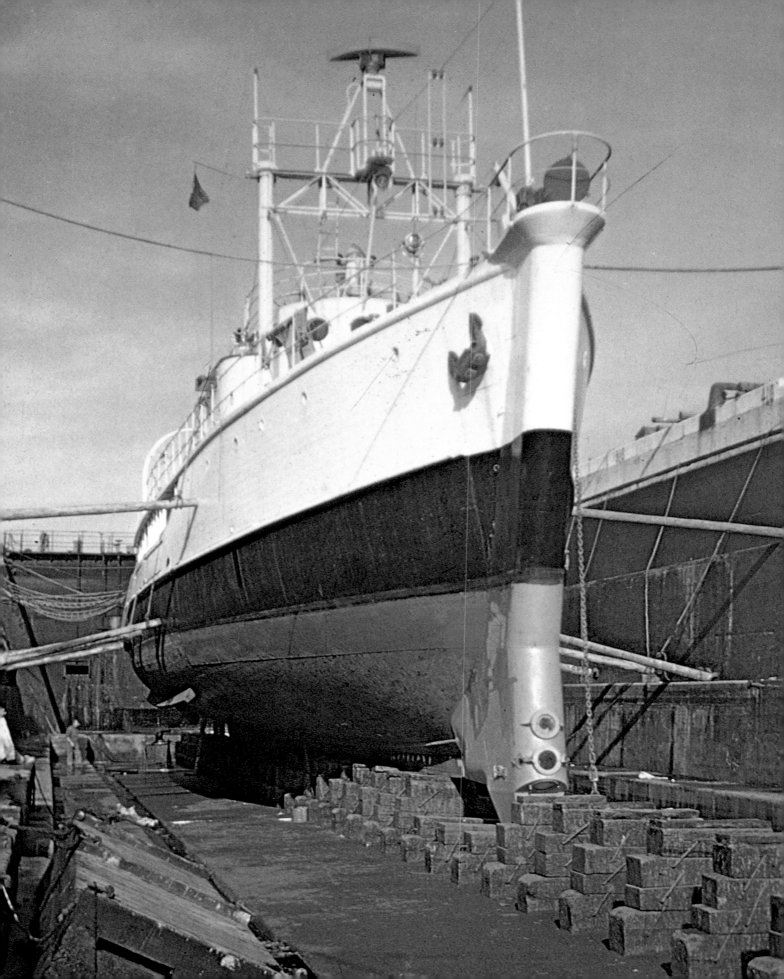

While alterations are in progress on the quarterdeck, Captain Saout and Engineer Mollard inspect the new hold panel.

amount of oxygen in the water in the immediate vicinity of the bottom. *Calypso* returns to Marseille on June 1st for an unexpected interlude. Wishing to give the first Eurovision program of its kind organized in France a special glamour, French Radio-Television decides to organize a broadcast called "Live from the Sea Floor" on the activities of the Cousteau team at one of their work sites.

Three main locations are chosen: the ancient ship at Grand Congloué; the Port of Marseille; and a modern sunken ship off the Island of Frioul.

The program is enlivened by celebrated contemporary commentators: Igor Barrère, Pierre Tchernia, Georges de Caunes, Roger Gouderc, and Alexandre Tarta. The program, the first of its kind in the world, is televised on June 15th, and scores a resounding success.

At Grand Congloué, for the first Eurovision program ever shown, Calypso is used as a base for the technicians. The mast of the "air lift" is used as a guide for the video cables.

Calypso in dry dock in Marseille. In the new false nose a room has been built to accommodate the sound transmitters.

On the quarterdeck of Calypso, moored above the wreck of Grand Congloué, television technicians adjust their cameras.
In the foreground, Alexis Sivirine, who took part in the program.

The Mysterious Gibraltar Currents

Calypso resumes her scientific functions without any time off. French participation in the International Geophysical Year provides for a study

Calypso, *her appearance considerably changed, is ready to carry on with new missions.*

in the field of oceanography of the distribution of Mediterranean waters that move westward along the bottom in the Strait of Gibraltar and flow into the Atlantic Ocean, where they slowly mix with the general circulation. The Phoenicians of antiquity knew about the rather unusual system of currents in the Strait of Gibraltar: Atlantic waters entering the Mediterranean create a powerful surface current running east, while a smaller quantity of Mediterranean water moves lower down along the Gibraltar shelf and creates a deep current running west. To leave the Mediterranean in spite of the surface current, the Phoenicians would sink a kind of large sail in deep water, unfurled like a parachute and ballasted, thus hauling their vessel towards the Atlantic. But how are these waters distributed? And how far do they flow? This is what Professor Lacombe will try to determine aboard *Calypso*.

On July 2d, a shipborne swell recorder and a

GEK electronic current recorder are installed aboard. Sampling water bottles will be lowered to conventional depths so that the Mediterranean waters circulating in the Atlantic can be identified by their temperature and salinity.

On July 12th, *Calypso* sails for the Atlantic under the command of Captain Jean Alinat, who replaces Captain Cousteau, passes Gibraltar on July 16th and arrives at Brest on the 20th. During a three months' voyage, often in heavy seas, *Calypso* accomplishes her program, calling at Vigo in Spain, at the Azores, in Tangier, and Lisbon.

The First Hull
of the Diving Saucer

During the summer months of that year, the ellipsoid hull of the future diving saucer is completed at OFRS, and on October 25th, *Calypso* takes it aboard. Heavily ballasted, it is submerged off the island of Riou and lowered to 2,000 feet on the end of a steel cable, including a strong braided nylon line to damp oscillation. The results of the tests are satisfactory.

Until the end of the year, *Calypso* devotes herself to a series of programs for various laboratories: she accompanies the bathyscaphe on a diving assignment during which she takes samples of plankton; she takes part in a sedimentology program; she dredges the ocean depths to collect special kinds of coral growing at depths of 1,000 to 2,600 feet in the Mediterranean; she makes microbiological studies; and finally, she takes some underwater photometric measurements.

A Crane Called "Yumbo"

Aware that the diving saucer was to weigh 8,140 pounds, Captain Cousteau had challenged OFRS to provide for equipment of some sort that could easily maneuver the heavy apparatus in rough seas without endangering the crew. He had been very impressed by a special boom used by the British in the Persian Gulf in 1954 that was able to place a sensitive gravimeter in the water and recover it without allowing it to swing from the end of the cable. Cousteau wanted the saucer to get quickly clamped to the crane's boom before it was removed from the water.

The miracle apparatus that seemed to fit the bill

is discovered at the Marseille Fair in September, 1957. It is a hydraulic crane with a 5-ton capacity used for public works and nicknamed "Yumbo." The construction engineer agrees to adapt it for maritime use. It was soon to revolutionize techniques for maneuvering equipment aboard ship and serve as a model for many other ships.

Yumbo is delivered to *Calypso* at the beginning

In Marseille harbor, the first hull made for the diving saucer is hoisted aboard Calypso *to undergo a series of tests.*

To test the hull, equipped with portholes this time, the saucer is lowered into the water by the hydraulic crane "Yumbo." Laban maneuvers the crane while Saout guides the minisub.

of January 1958. *Calypso*'s wooden deck is reinforced and the crane, positioned aft on portside, will be able to lift the saucer from the sea either from the rear or from the side of the ship.

The Saucer Is Lost

In March, OFRS finishes fitting the saucer with its observation portholes and with strain gauges to measure the stress in various parts of the hull under pressure.

On March 19th, the saucer, loaded with one and a half tons of ballast, is lowered by *Calypso* to a depth of 2,000 feet. The boatswain maneuvers the winch cautiously to avoid jerking the cable too violently. The ascent is taking place without difficulty when suddenly, as the saucer nears the surface, the ship veers sharply. The cable snaps and lashes about on the quarterdeck like a giant whip. The accident could have been a tragic one, but fortunately only one person is slightly injured—Raymond Coll, who escapes with a superficial cut on his cheek.

Calypso returns to the same spot the next day. The graph of the highly accurate echo sounder indicates that the diving saucer is floating 33 feet above its ballast at a depth of 3,280 feet. The

portholes and hull have withstood the pressure even better than expected.

Alas! The difficulty of dredging at that depth is obvious and salvaging the saucer is suspended. *Calypso* departs again for a dozen new research programs involving hydrology, seismology, geology, and biology, off Marseille, Nice, and Corsica. It is between two of these missions that Cousteau, examining some precisions sonar recordings, notices a few remarkable hills at a depth of 8,500 feet—he describes them at a Congress of Geology in Villefranche and later on, with Alinat, interprets them as salt domes ... beacons for possible oil deposits in the deep waters of the Mediterranean. On June 26th, *Calypso* loads the equipment to be used during a joint hydrological-biological program with naturalists from Monaco, Marseille, and Paris.

Lisbon, Porto, Ceuta, Madeira and Alborán are ports of call in a long journey that will continue via Tangier, Palma, and Barcelona. During a dredging operation at Alborán, a variety of kelp is brought aboard. Its stem is more than six and a half feet long and its large leaves more than a foot wide. Falco dives and discovers a large forest of these kelp at depths of 130 to 140 feet. He recommends a return to the site whenever possible.

Hoisting a troika aboard.

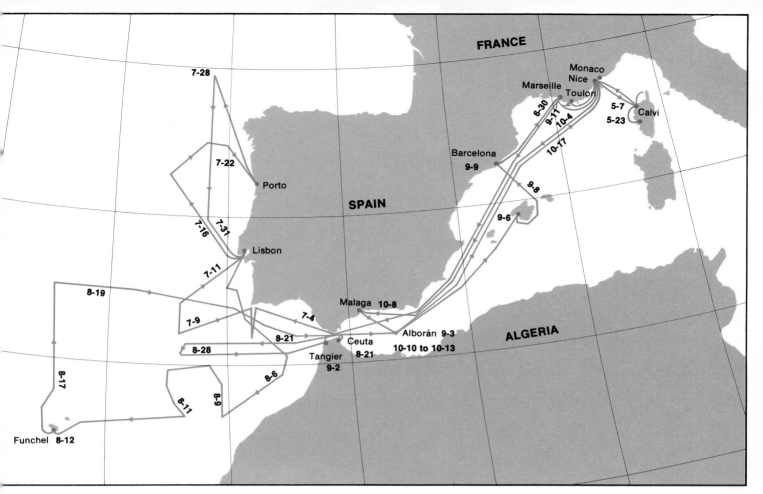

1958

The Poor Man's
Bathyscaphe

On September 23d, *Calypso* tests a new invention: a photographic sledge designed to be towed on the bottom of the sea. It is christened the "troika" because its top arch looks like that of a Russian sled.

The idea first came to Cousteau during one of his dives in the bathyscaphe FNRS III, while at a depth of 4,900 feet. Though he was fascinated by the bathyscaphe's potential for exploration, Cousteau was well aware of the considerable costs involved in its operation. *Calypso* was much too small to add on such a heavy and cumbersome vehicle but at the same time she did need to obtain photographs and even films from the deepest seas. Hence the troika, a strange construction of tubes able to be towed to depths of more than 25,000 feet and equipped with automatic Edgerton cameras and flash. The device was designed in such a way that even if it tipped over while being towed, the cable's traction would right it to its normal position on two runners.

It is indeed a new tool that *Calypso* has offered to the oceanographic community. In the years to come, the troikas would take tens of thousands of valuable photographs in deep waters.

On October 4th, *Calypso* returns to the island of Alborán for more extensive diving among the large kelp discovered in August by Falco. The superb forest of laminaria, whose height reaches 20 to 26 feet, extends for over half a mile, at a depth of 131 feet. It looks somewhat like a plantation of banana trees. Large silver leerfish circle above the forest in schools; scorpion fish lurk under the vegetation. A film is shot at this magnificent site.

On October 27th, a new study of plankton begins off the coasts of Nice, Cannes, and Genoa, with Professor Trégouboff. Then Gaz de France, the French National Gas Company, proposes a new project to Captain Cousteau: a thorough study of the possibilities of laying gas pipelines at depths of more than 7,000 feet to bring natural gas from Algeria to Spain and to supply most of Europe.

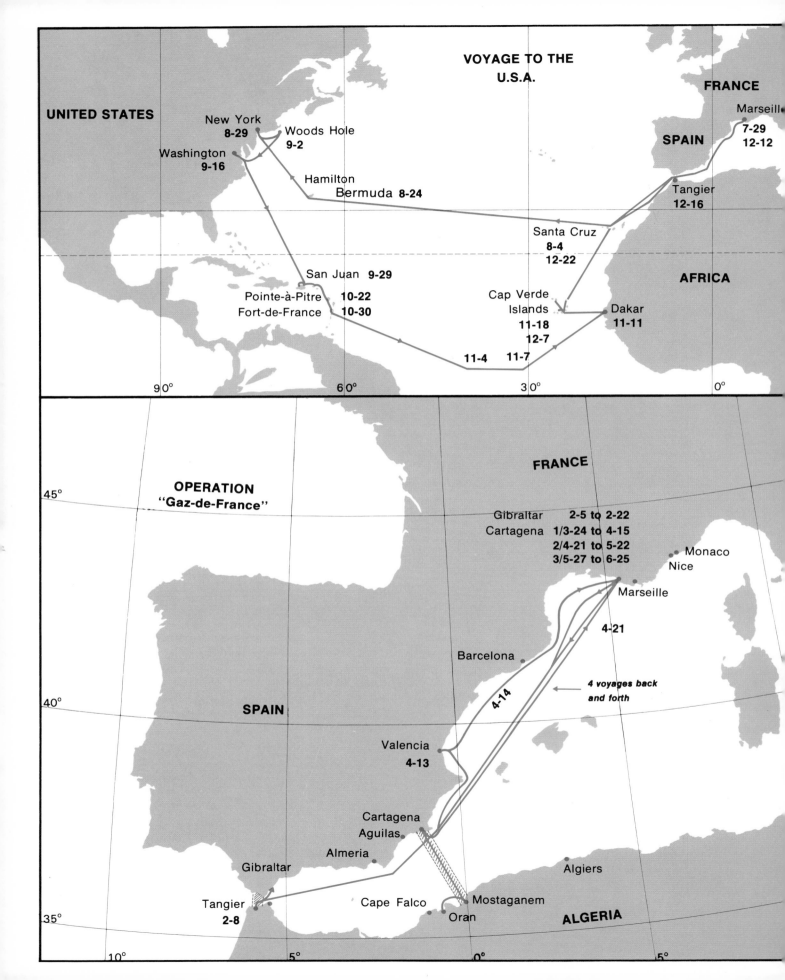

VOYAGE TO THE U.S.A.

UNITED STATES

New York **8-29**
Woods Hole **9-2**
Washington **9-16**
Hamilton
Bermuda **8-24**

San Juan **9-29**
Pointe-à-Pitre **10-22**
Fort-de-France **10-30**

11-4   **11-7**

FRANCE
Marseille **7-29** **12-12**

SPAIN

Tangier **12-16**

Santa Cruz **8-4** **12-22**

Cap Verde Islands **11-18** **12-7**

Dakar **11-11**

AFRICA

90°   60°   30°   0°

OPERATION "Gaz-de-France"

FRANCE

Gibraltar   **2-5 to 2-22**
Cartagena   **1/3-24 to 4-15**
             2/4-21 to 5-22
             3/5-27 to 6-25

Monaco
Nice

Marseille

4-21

45°

Barcelona

4 voyages back and forth

4-14

40°

SPAIN

Valencia **4-13**

Cartagena
Aguilas
Almeria

Gibraltar

Tangier **2-8**   Cape Falco   Mostaganem   Algiers

Oran   ALGERIA

35°

10°   5°   0°   5°

By a secondary transceiver station at Cape Falco, Calypso *with her antenna and all the radio equipment.*

1959

Of Gas in the Water

The Soil of the Ocean

From January 1959 on, frequent discussions are held aboard ship with experts and technicians from Gaz de France. The task is to organize the broadest and most accurate study of deepwater topography ever done to date. It is a very important one because the route that is selected will determine if and where the pipelines between Spain and North Africa can be submerged later on.

Obviously marine charts cannot be relied upon. Underwater transoceanic cables can be submerged almost at random, but laying steel pipes on the sea floor that are to function under high pressure requires extensive knowledge of even the slightest irregularity of the bottom, corrosion factors such as dissolved oxygen and anaerobic bacteria, and the mechanical resistance of the soil.

Commandant Cousteau, with Commandant Alinat by his side, maneuvers the crane Yumbo as the diving saucer is hoisted on board, July 26, 1959.

Taking along the diving saucer, troikas, antishark cage, and various other apparatus, Calypso leaves Marseille on July 29, 1959, and heads for the U.S.A.

It is decided to verify first the reliability of the studies already made on the shortest underwater route—i.e., across the Strait of Gibraltar. On February 5th, *Calypso* arrives in Tangier. Captain Saout is in command; Captain Alinat is on board with technicians from Gaz de France. After a week of difficult work, all the required soundings have been made. *Calypso* sails for Marseille in heavy seas.

Analysis of the results reveals that the route is not a desirable one. It is decided to study another one, this time between Mostaganem in Algeria and Cartagena in Spain— a distance of about 112 miles— at a depth reaching 7,870 feet.

Calypso's sonar system is capable of measuring depths to within a foot, and obtaining information on the consistency of the top $6\frac{1}{2}$ to 10 feet of sediment. But this information is useful only if the ship's position is accurately known within a few yards. Captain Cousteau calls upon the most modern technology of that time. The network selected is a "Decca two range" system. The main transmitting station is installed on board *Calypso*, while the secondary transceivers, called "slaves," are set up ashore on both sides of the Mediterranean—the "green" one is at Aguilas, near Cartagena, and the "red" one is at Cape Falco, near Oran. A 45-foot antenna is erected on an insulated base on the quarterdeck and secured on all sides by braces crisscrossed with insulators. A copper grating covers the quarterdeck. The system gives positions accurate to within 33 feet during the day and 98 feet at night. This is judged sufficient to pinpoint every obstacle. On the bridge a plotter automatically traces the course followed by *Calypso*.

Calypso leaves Marseille for Cartagena on March 24th, with Captain Alinat as skipper. Captain Cousteau is occupied with administrative problems and can only be aboard ship at intervals. Hundreds of stations are made during the course of endless shuttles between Algeria and Spain. Besides mapping the area, *Calypso* also dredges, takes cores, bottom samples, measures the oxygen content of the water just one inch above the bottom sediment, draws bacterial cultures from the mud, and finally, and most important, takes thousands of photographs with the troika at great depths as it is towed over hundreds of miles.

On June 25th, the final fixes are taken, and after celebrating with champagne, the team returns to Marseille. The data are analyzed in Monaco, Marseille, and Paris. A channel has been found

PROPERTY OF
MATTITUCK HIGH SCHOOL
LIBRARY

where gas pipelines can be safely laid from Algeria to Spain. However, political reasons led Algiers to prefer transport of the gas in liquid form.

The Diving Saucer Is Christened

On July 25th, after being careened, repainted and overhauled, *Calypso* christens her brand new small, two-man exploration submarine, called the *soucoupe plongeante S.P. 350*. The event takes place in Marseille in the presence of the Secretary for Merchant Marine. The saucer is perfectly watertight and responds beautifully to command. This initial dive with Jean Mollard and Albert Falco at the controls is the first in a long series— as these words are being printed, the saucer is 18 years old, 975 dives have been made and she is still going strong! The revolutionary minisub without propeller becomes one of *Calypso*'s indispensable tools from the month of July on. She completely changes the way in which underwater exploration is carried out and assures man's active presence in the sea at depths of up to 1,150 feet.

Photographs of Continental Drift:

Since *Calypso* had to be in New York on September 1, 1959, for the first World Oceanographic Congress, Cousteau organizes an expedition for the occasion—an exploration of the flat top and of the slopes of several seamounts (guyots) and further along the bottom and inner walls of the famous Atlantic Rift Valley. The expedition is to be carried out with a team of biologists from Marseille and by geologist Lloyd Breslau, using dredges and troikas.

Calypso sails from Marseille on July 29th. After calling at Santa Cruz, on the island of Tenerife in the Canaries, *Calypso* steers a course west. The seamounts she will explore are truncated volcanic coves rising from the abyssal plain, more than 15,000 feet deep, up to 330 to 1,000 feet. *Calypso* submerges a brand new kind of stationary reference point by moving "kytoons" on the shallow top of the seamounts as well as in the middle of the Atlantic Rift Valley (7,544 feet). The kytoon is a streamlined balloon filled with helium, somewhat similar to the "sausage" balloons of World

At sea, engineers Mollard and Laban give the diving saucer a last-minute checking.

War I. It is inflated on board and anchored by a thin nylon line to a grapnel of about 44 pounds. It carries a light aluminum foil radar target. Using radar, *Calypso* takes her bearings relative to the balloon and is thus able to adjust her speed relative to the bottom despite the currents. This is necessary because the troikas, which take 600 pairs of color stereo photographs during each

A "Kytoon" is going to be launched and tied to the line of its grapnel, already anchored. It will be a stationary reference point on the sea.

One of the 600 stereoscopic photographs taken underwater in 1959 on the Mid-Atlantic Ridge.

operation, must be towed along the bottom at a ground speed of less than two knots.

Although one of *Calypso*'s troikas was lost during the course of the program amid the chaos of the deep-lying rocks of the Mid-Atlantic Ridge, thousands of photographs of the greatest scientific importance were brought back.

A Spectacular Welcome in New York

After a stopover in the Bermudas, *Calypso* arrives in New York on August 29th, the evening before the opening of the congress. Her welcome is spectacular: an escort of hooting tugboats, waterworks from the fireboats, sirens from ships and docks make a deafening noise, while a dirigible hovers in the sky taking pictures—little *Calypso* receives the same kind of welcome from New York as the *Normandie* or the *Queen Mary* on her maiden voyage.

During the sessions of the Oceanographic Congress, Captain Cousteau shows and comments on the extraordinary photographs just taken in the mid-Atlantic.

On *Calypso*, city officials, navy representatives, scientists, visitors, journalists, and photographers file aboard by the thousands.

After these warm demonstrations, *Calypso* sails to the renowned Oceanographic Institute at Woods Hole, then travels up the Potomac as far as Washington, where she is a grateful guest of the National Geographic Society.

Photographing the Deepest Trench in the Atlantic

The ship sets out for France again at an unhurried pace. September is the month of tropical cyclones, but it is also a time of calm periods favorable for difficult operations at sea. *Calypso* attempts to tow the troika, equipped with Edgerton cameras and flash, along the bottom of the Puerto Rico Trench, 26,240 feet below the surface and the deepest trench in all the Atlantic. The new winch has an enormous drum and is supplied with 40,000 feet of steel cable of progressive strength. To take good photographs, the ship must move at a speed of approximately one mile per hour. Here again, because of varying currents, surface

August 29, 1959—triumphal welcome to Calypso in New York.

speed cannot be relied upon, and a beacon is necessary.

Cousteau tries anchoring one of the kytoons on a thin nylon line, five miles long with a buoy at the surface. But three times running, the rope is cut by some mysterious creature, later identified as a shark, and the principle of the kytoon is abandoned! However, with some acrobatic maneuvering, several series of 600 photographs of the trench's bottom are taken, revealing numerous traces of life.

On Fire beneath the Sea

Although the diving saucer's shape is a purely logical one, it irresistibly invokes comparisons with the extraterrestrial flying saucers in the world of science fiction. But the saucer is real, and proves herself operational. Her first actual dive takes place near the western coast of Puerto Rico. She is then seriously put to the test at Guadaloupe,

off Pigeon Island. Unfortunately, the cadmium-nickel batteries that energize the saucer are not properly insulated; an underwater explosion, which occurs while Falco is piloting the saucer and Professor Edgerton is aboard as passenger, puts the trials to a stop

Calypso sets out for home but continues to take soundings as well as photographs with the troika. On November 11, 1959, she is in Dakar where Doctor Jacques Forest embarks to lead a very important study of the marine fauna of the Cape Verde Islands

A new set of cadmium-nickel batteries for the saucer arrives by plane in the Cape Verde Islands and she resumes diving. But during a dive with Falco and Cousteau, another explosion forces the team to jettison the lead emergency weight and return to the surface. Mollard decides to change the type of batteries and to use more conventional lead cells and that puts an end to the trouble.

On December 25th, *Calypso* arrives in Toulon, where she remains in port until January 22, 1960.

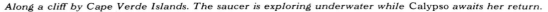

Along a cliff by Cape Verde Islands. The saucer is exploring underwater while Calypso *awaits her return.*

The art and the technique of lifting the diving saucer from the hold with the crane Yumbo.

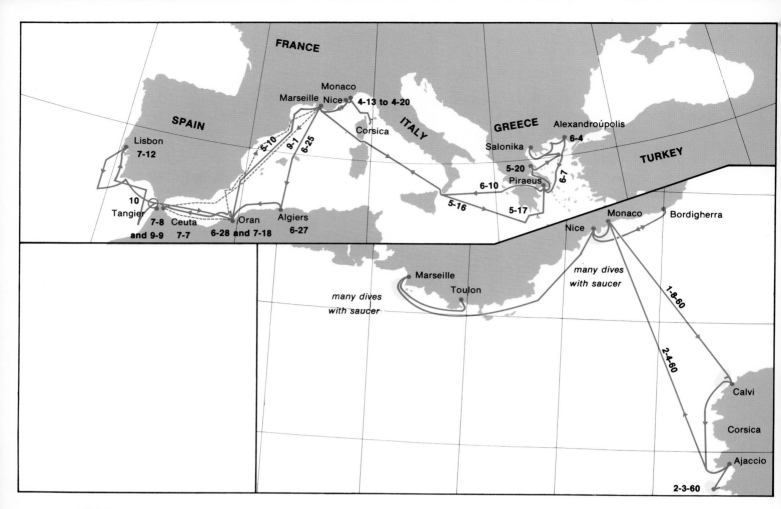

1960

Mediterranean Programs

The month of January, 1960, is marked by the departure of Captain François Saout. He retires after nine years of service aboard *Calypso* on the sea-lanes of the world. Captain Alinat replaces him as interim skipper for the first expeditions of the new year.

Calypso takes the diving saucer on board at Marseille. Professor Pérès then embarks in Monaco and the ship is headed for Calvi and Ajaccio, where the diving saucer is to be used several times to a depth of one-thousand feet. Falco is at the controls. His first passenger is Captain Cousteau, the second one Professor Pérès. The structure of the steep canyons that dent the continental

shelf of western Corsica is studied in detail. During these dives, the saucer observes several octopi that lived in a corner of quasi-rectangular gardens bordered by enclosing walls they had built with whatever stones, pieces of pottery, or debris they had found in the vicinity.

On April 11th, *Calypso* welcomes aboard her new captain, Roger Maritano, who will be in command for eight years.

For the rest of the year, *Calypso* undertakes many scientific programs with Doctor Romanovsky: a study made both with current meters and with troikas in an attempt to correlate the velocity of currents with ripple marks at Villefranche, Corisca, and off the coast of Elba; with Professor Bourcart, corings, soundings, and seismic profiles made with the help of Edgerton's "thumper" and "boomer," two new high-intensity sound transmitters; and with Professor Trégouboff, specimens of fish and samples of plankton are taken.

From Greece to North Africa

Calypso leaves again, this time bound for Greece on a program directed by Professor Pérès. Dredgings and photographic profiles with the troika are made in the Matapan Trench deeper than thirteen-thousand feet. Standard hydrology and soundings are done in collaboration with Greek scientists along the Euboea Channel, Volos, Līmnos, Thessalonika, Alexandroúpolis, Piraeus, and the Gulf of Corinth.

Calypso returns to Marseille and other programs follow: hydrology off the coast of Algiers with Professor Ivanoff; studies of radioactivity in the western Mediterranean—often in heavy seas; collecting specimens of fish and plankton at Ville-franche, in collaboration with the bathyscaphe FNRS III; a geological program with Bourcart between Corsica and the coasts of Nice and Bordighera.

From September 1st to October 6th, an important expedition with Professor Lacombe takes *Calypso* off the coast of Cape Spartel in Morocco for electromagnetic current measurements with a GEK and hydrology research.

On the way back, Captain Alinat, in collaboration with Gaz de France, lays several hundred yards of experimental pipes similar to those selected for the natural gas project, along the route of the proposed Mostaganem-Cartegena pipeline. They will remain underwater for one year for a study of corrosion.

In October, *Calypso* serves as tender for the saucer and tests "explosive anchors" which plant themselves deep in the ocean floor, to provide more secure anchorages.

Finally, on December 10th, *Calypso* is in Nice for the launching of a monstrous Zodiac, a 480 horsepower, 66 foot long and 25 foot wide inflatable ship designed by Cousteau. She is the world's largest inflatable boat. Princess Grace christens her *Amphitrite* and after the ceremony, she and Prince Rainer are received aboard *Calypso*.

Thanks to the hydraulic crane, the diving saucer is launched safely. A diver stands ready to untie the minisub as soon as it is submerged.

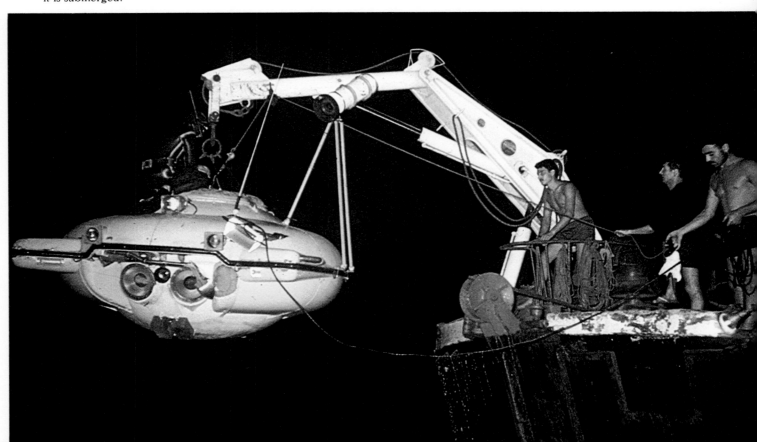

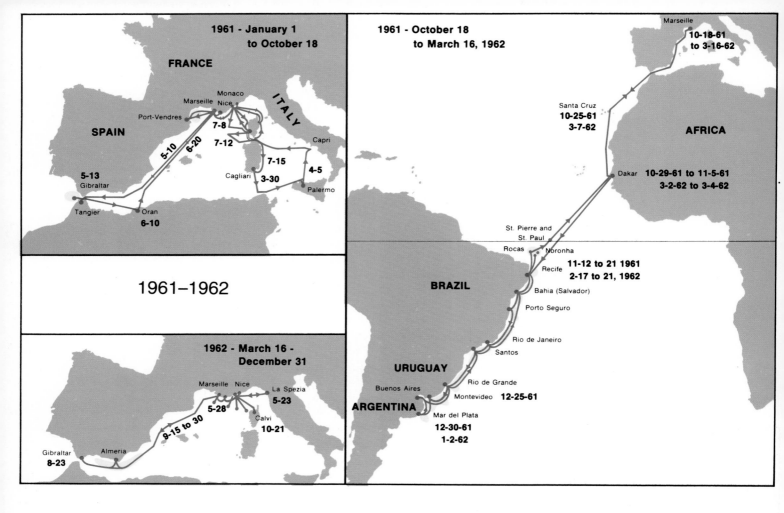

1961–1962

1961 - January 1 to October 18

FRANCE
ITALY
SPAIN

Marseille
Monaco
Nice
Port-Vendres

7-8
7-12
7-15
Capri
Cagliari
3-30
4-5
Palermo

5-10
6-20

5-13
Gibraltar

Tangier
Oran
6-10

1961 - October 18 to March 16, 1962

Marseille
10-18-61
to 3-16-62

Santa Cruz
10-25-61
3-7-62

AFRICA

Dakar   10-29-61 to 11-5-61
3-2-62 to 3-4-62

St. Pierre and St. Paul
Rocas
Noronha
Recife   11-12 to 21 1961
2-17 to 21, 1962

BRAZIL

Bahia (Salvador)
Porto Seguro

Rio de Janeiro
Santos

URUGUAY

Buenos Aires
Rio de Grande
Montevideo   12-25-61

ARGENTINA

Mar del Plata
12-30-61
1-2-62

1962 - March 16 - December 31

Marseille
Nice
La Spezia
5-23

5-28
Calvi
10-21

9-15 to 30

Gibraltar
8-23
Almeria

Atlantic Programs

The Year of the Saucer

The year 1961 begins with the forty-first dive of the saucer. Albert Falco and J. Picard take her down near Riou Island off the coast of Marseille. The year will be a very busy one for the saucer, as many scientific organizations want to avail themselves of her for their work. The saucer reaches a depth of 985 feet at Cape Bear on Rech Lacaze Duthiers. Miss Devon, a biologist from Port-Vendres and the first woman to be taken down, is along on the saucer's fiftieth dive.

On February 9th, *Calypso* is back in the Marseille dockyard, but, from the 28th on, the ship carries out many coring programs around Nice.

On March 5th, *Calypso* and her team welcome the famous American oceanography ship *Atlantis* to Monaco. Then she sails immediately with a program of geological studies that require the combined use of the saucer down to 1,000 feet and of drop-corers for greater depths—up to 7,330 feet in the area of Port-Vendres and Cape Creus. A program of photometry with Ivanoff follows immediately—in Sardinia, on the coast of Tunisia, and in Sicily. *Calypso* returns via Capri and the Strait of Bonifacio.

Then it's off on another geological program with the Edgerton thumper in the vicinity of Marseille. Diving with the saucer in the clear waters of Corsica with Falco and Laban follows to check the efficiency of the saucer's horizontal sonar. Operation Lumen follows, led by Captain Cousteau himself, undertaken to measure the transparency of open-sea water horizontally at various depths. A 500-watt lamp attached to a sonar target is lowered under *Calypso;* the saucer, equipped with a recording photomultiplier, is suspended at the same depth as the lamp under a launch by a nylon cable and distance from lamp to saucer is increased slowly until the light is no longer perceived. The transparency is found to be maximum at the depth of 825 feet, when the lamp would still be perceived at a distance of 1,000 feet.

On May 8th, with Professor Lacombe, *Calypso* participates in an international program of continuous current measurements on the Atlantic side of the Strait of Gibraltar, together with the ships *Origny, Hellen, Hansen, Stafetta,* and *Eupen*. Bad weather, and even a storm, mark this expedition as a painful one for the participants. Upon her return, *Calypso* carries out two more programs. Bottom populations are studied south of Nice by the *Winaretta Singer,* a ship from the Oceanographic Institute of Monaco, using the

In a bay at Frioul, an island off Marseille, the crew of Calypso *is installing the first house under the sea, Conshelf I. Falco, on the surface, controls and operation.*

Technical Hardships

Calypso sails for Santa Cruz on the island of Tenerife on October 18th in very rough seas. En route, we notice that the bow hold is filling with water. After several inspections, we find that the sea cock of one of the toilet pipes that had been changed before departure is leaking badly. Since it cannot be repaired at sea, we pump the water out until we reach Santa Cruz. Once there, we look for a shipyard, but in vain. We pump all the way to Dakar, where *Calypso* arrives on October 30th.

The repair is made quickly, but a more serious problem arises: water is leaking onto the starboard engine. Engineer Jacques Picard comes out from Monaco and decides to patch up the hole with a special cement. Relying on this precarious repair, *Calypso* begins the long transatlantic journey from Dakar to Recife, Brazil, a distance of 1,800 miles.

Exploring Undersea Pampas

On November 8th, *Calypso* crosses the equator for the fourth time and ritual dunkings are given by Maurice Léandri to all those crossing the line for the first time. She enters the Port of Recife on November 11th.

A Franco-Brazilian team of five biologists embarks at Recife and the expedition begins on November 16th.

For a period of a month and a half, *Calypso* takes samples, by dredging, trawling, and diving, of the flora and fauna at 184 locations between Recife and Mar del Plata in Argentina. Plankton is also collected. Before the *Calypso* expedition, little was known of the biology of the Brazilian continental shelf, and no data was available on the ecology of marine communities.

Recife, Rocas, Bahia (Salvador), Porto Seguro, Rio de Janeiro, Santos, Rio Grande, Montevideo (where *Calypso* spends Christmas with Captain and Mrs. Cousteau who have come over from Europe), Mar del Plata (reached on December 30th, at 7:55 P.M.) are the ports of call on this expedition.

Professor Forest and his assistants leave *Calypso* in Buenos Aires on January 16th; they are immediately replaced by the team of Professor Pérès. Again *Calypso* skirts the coast of South America, taking innumerable samples of fish,

In the Atlantic Ocean, off the Strait of Gibraltar, moored at great depth in rough seas, Calypso *and* Hellen Hansen *are carrying on a hydrological mission.*

Courage and skill were always the main characteristics of the crew. Here Octave Léandri and René Robino are repairing a clutch.

troika to supplement classic instruments. Thereafter, with atomic scientists from Saclay, *Calypso* measures the amount of radioactivity in the water and in sediments between Nice and Corsica. This routine work comes to an end on July 18th so that *Calypso* can make preparations for a long expedition of six months to South America.

76

crustaceans, shells, and fixed fauna and flora from the continental shelf at hundreds of stations. The scientific tasks are thoroughly carried out despite all the hardship *Calypso* had to endure: on January 10th, the main starboard engine fails; on the 13th, the clutch for the port engine shows signs of wear; on January 26th, after a hard day's work in a rough sea, the electric board is flooded, causing a total power failure aboard ship and a threat of fire; on January 30th, a rubber connecting hose from the starboard generator bursts and floods the engine. The oil tanks are polluted and 208 gallons of oil have to be disposed of. What's more, the motor for one of the fire pumps in flooded. On February 8th at 7 A.M., the portside generator burns out completely. At 9 P.M. there is an oil leak in the main starboard engine that spills 52 gallons of oil into the hold.

The mechanics were able to make the necessary repairs as each bit of bad luck fell on them and the ship was never diverted from her scientific work.

On February 17th, the scientists fly back from Recife, repairs are made, supplies are replenished, and on February 21st, *Calypso* tackles the 1,800 mile Atlantic crossing.

After sailing past Noronha, Rocas and Saint Paul's Rocks, *Calypso* arrives in Dakar on March 2d. The ship passes by Santa Cruz on Tenerife on March 7th, and later seeks shelter in the Bay of Rosas, Spain, because of extremely bad weather. As *Calypso* leaves Rosas, she loses her port anchor. She searches for it, finds it, set out again, and finishes the 16,350-mile-long expedition in Marseille on March 16th.

Learning the Sea the Hard Way

Calypso should have been entitled to a period of calm and a time for repairs. Not so! Programs have already been set up and, being the only French oceanographic vessel in existence at the time, she has to leave on new assignments.

Sixteen programs will occupy her time from May 6th to October 30th. Careening and major repairs have to wait until November and the port engine will therefore have to operate at 800 rpm instead of 920 for six months. Here is a brief summary of her schedule:

—May 12th to 15th: sediment coring off Villefranche

—May 20th to 28th: hydrology for the international marine radioactivity lab off La Spezia

—June 1st to 12th: major program of seismic refraction between Nice and Corsica.

At one point, *Calypso* is a veritable powder keg with 52 depth charges of 297, 220, and 77 pounds aboard, enough to sink herself along with the *Espadon* and the *Winaretta Singer,* ships from the Museum of Oceanography who are working with her. It is the first time Cousteau witnesses the

With the folding arm in front of the false nose, Calypso is ready to work with the "thumper."

massive use of explosives for geophysics. He understands the damage done to marine life and from then on fights to have TNT replaced by less destructive pressure wave generators.

— June 16th to 26th: soundings and troika photography along the French coast
— June 27th to 29th: geophysics and inspection of canyons off the coast of Esterel.

During her stay in Marseille, *Calypso's* team challenges Monaco to a game of soccer that had been planned for quite a while. After the match, the players and their families gather aboard ship. It is night time and no one is watching the children. One of the kids falls between the ship and the wharf, in immediate danger of being crushed; Falco, who saw what happened, jumps into the water fully clothed and manages to bring the child up safe and sound.

— July 2d to 10th: seismic profiling off La Ciotat
— July 16th to 24th: seismic refraction
— July 26th to 30th: hydrology and geology
— August 3d to 12th: sediment coring in deep water.

This series of assignments is carried out with the RANA, a new radio-navigation system, enabling *Calypso,* for many years, to determine her position in a radius of 200 miles around Monaco, within a few yards.

From August 13th to the 29th, *Calypso* is on a special acoustics program with Professor René-Guy Busnel, head of the Physiological Acoustics Laboratory of the CNRS in Jouy-en-Josas. The various sounds—clicks, pops, and whistles—of marine mammals (dolphins and pilot whales) are recorded and analyzed in the Strait of Gibraltar, where cetaceans abound, swimming in and out of the Mediterranean. Whenever the sounds recorded are played back to another group of mammals, the effect is instantaneous: there is a general stampede.

The First House under the Sea

No one is a prophet in his own land. Doctor George Bond, M.D., U.S. Navy, had conceived a "saturation diving" method to increase the effi-

ciency of dives and recommended to the navy that it test his theory with gas-filled shelters, "houses under the sea." He was not listened to. With Bond's bitter consent, Cousteau decided to devote *Calypso* to the "Conshelf program" and "Conshelf I" was tested in September 1962. The program was conservative: "Two men living for one week in a small dwelling at a depth of 37 feet and working several hours a day at 65 feet." Conshelf I, developed by OFRS, was a simple, heavily ballasted cylinder, equipped with an open hatch at the lower part. In memory of the tub inhabited by the Greek philosopher, the contraption is christened *Diogenes.*

On September 14th *Calypso* tows *Diogenes* to a small bay at Frioul, an island off Marseille, and carefully submerges the structure on the selected site. The first two "oceanauts" in history, Albert Falco and Claude Wesly, swim down to their home in the presence of many journalists and photographers who watch them settle in on closed circuit television.

According to plans, the oceanauts leave their home several hours a day to work at 65 feet. Though rather cramped for space in *Diogenes,* the oceanauts were equipped with radio and television. They also received many visitors: Captain Cousteau, Professor Chouteau, Dr. Fructus, and even a newspaper reporter. They were daily submitted to various physiological tests. After breathing oxygen for an hour to avoid potential decompression accidents, they finally surfaced, in perfect condition, on September 21st. A new frontier in the conquest of the sea had been crossed.

More conventional programs headed by various specialists in the general area between Corsica and the coast of Provence are:

— September 24th to 30th: seismic profiling and tests of Edgerton's "mud penetrator," a device that picks out hard objects and rocks buried in sediment
— October 1st to 4th: radio chemistry of seawater
— October 5th to 25th: hydrology and current measurements.

Calypso finally returns to Toulon where the long-awaited careening and general overhaul can at last be done.

Cousteau gives his instructions for a delicate maneuver: the mooring of the cylinder that will become a house under the sea.

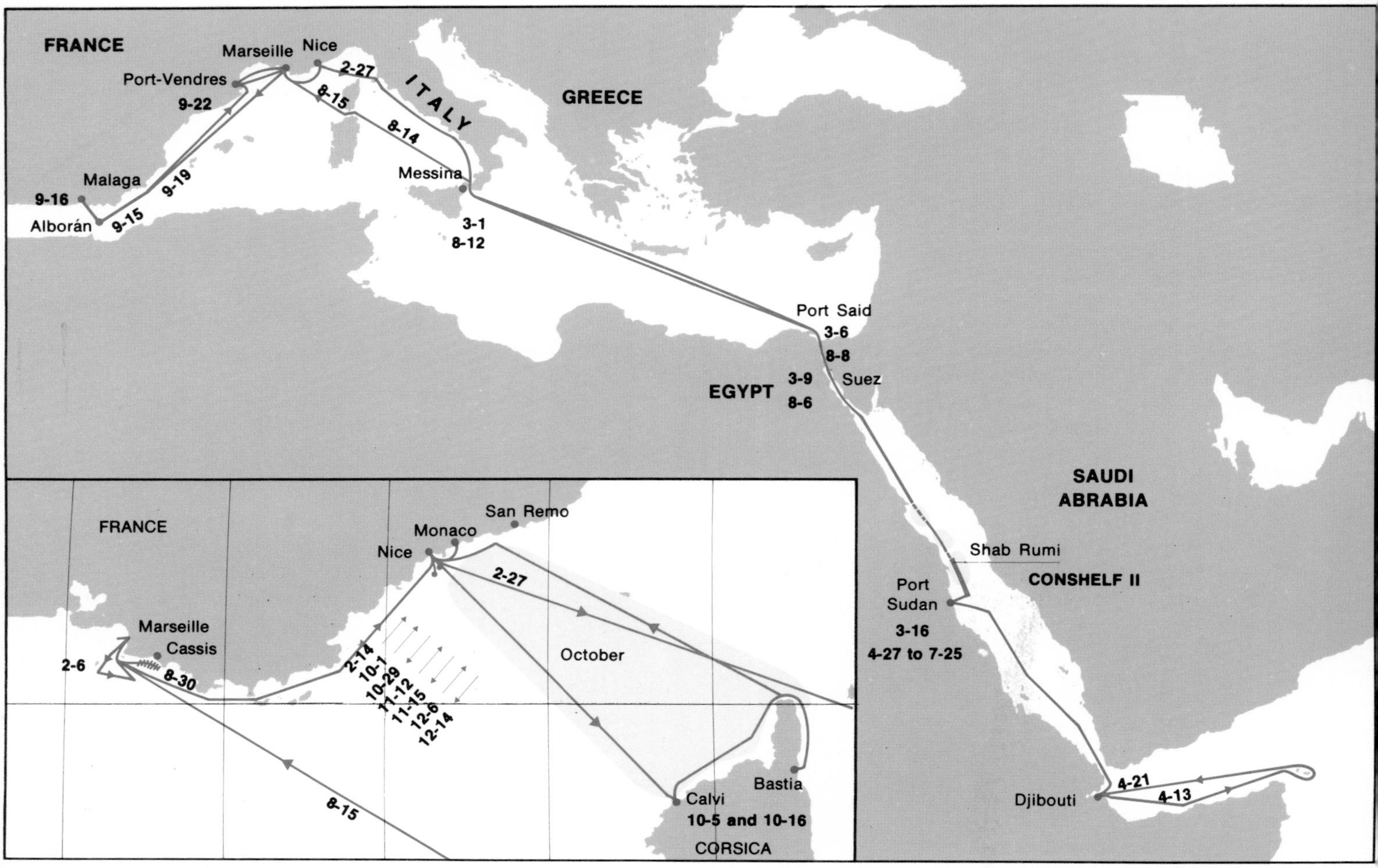
FRANCE
Marseille
Nice
Port-Vendres
2-27
ITALY
GREECE
9-22
8-15
8-14
Malaga
Messina
9-19
9-16
Alborán
9-15
3-1
8-12
Port Said
3-6
8-8
3-9
Suez
EGYPT
8-6
SAUDI
ABRABIA
Shab Rumi
CONSHELF II
Port
Sudan
3-16
4-27 to 7-25
Djibouti
4-21
4-13
FRANCE
San Remo
Monaco
Nice
2-27
Marseille
Cassis
October
2-6
8-30
2-14
10-1
10-29
11-12
11-15
12-6
12-14
Bastia
Calvi
10-5 and 10-16
CORSICA
8-15

1963

At Home in the Sea for a Month

In Port Sudan, Rosaldo *and* Calypso *are ready to tow the underwater houses out to Shab Rumi.*

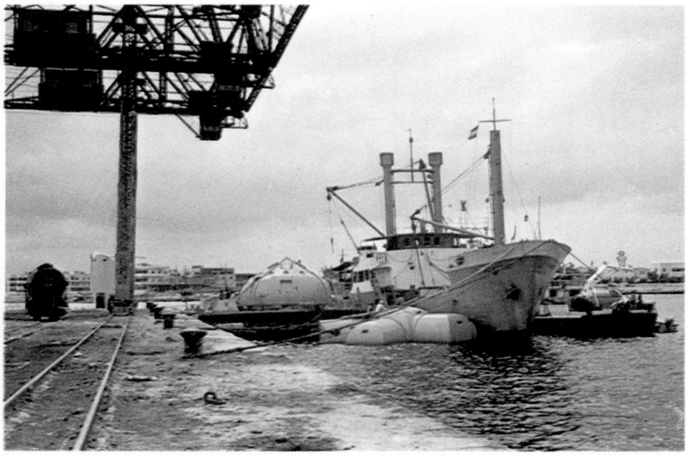

Setting Up a Challenging Experiment

Drawing a lesson from the successful operation of Conshelf I, the day after the experiment ended, Captain Cousteau decided to set up a second more ambitious project, "Conshelf II," designed to demonstrate that important scientific or industrial undersea operations could be undertaken far away from the home base. The project had three technical goals: (*a*) to study the effects of a month-long stay at 33 feet with work done at 60 feet; (*b*) to study the effects of a week-long stay at 82 feet inside a dwelling filled with an air-helium mixture, actual work being performed daily at 160 feet or more; and (*c*) to install an undersea garage for the saucer where she might be overhauled and reloaded without having to surface. Together the "buildings" were to form a veritable underwater village, set up in the Red Sea.

As always, financing was the real adventure. No

conventional source of funds could be obtained for such a daring and expensive project. Cousteau then turns to his best friend, cinema, and succeeds in obtaining a generous contract to produce a feature-length film of the expedition called *World Without Sun*. But the real accomplishment is that the final decision is made in October, 1962 and *Calypso* is ready to leave on February 27, 1963. All the houses, hangars, accessories and instruments needed for Conshelf II are ready to leave Nice on April 10th aboard the Italian freighter *Rosaldo,* chartered especially for the occasion!

Looking for an Improbable Site

On February 27th, *Calypso* sails for Port Said and the Red Sea. Two preliminary tasks are at hand: to shoot spectacular film footage with the saucer and to find the best location for Operation Conshelf II, scheduled to get under way in May.

Roger Maritano is still *Calypso's* captain. Simone Cousteau and Captain Cousteau are on board. After passing the Suez Canal, the team examines and films innumerable reefs in search of a suitable site for the experiment. A reef must be found, rising from greater depths like a staircase, with ledges at 33 and 82 feet, sheltered from the prevailing winds. The water must be clear and crowded with fish. All these conditions are not easy to meet simultaneously!

Calypso visits Shab Ali, Daedulus, Elba, Musa, Khebi, Baracut, Dzeberjed and Shab Aubier. On March 26th, thanks to a friend in Port Sudan, Mohammed Ali, the site is found—Shab Rumi, located 27 miles north of Port Sudan beyond the Sanganeb Lighthouse.

Calypso then uses available time to shoot underwater sequences for the film, visiting dozens of reefs south of Port Sudan; she passes the Strait of Bab el Mandeb and calls in Djibouti. She heads east in the Gulf of Aden and the Sea of Oman all the way to Socotra Island and then returns to Port Sudan via Djibouti. She meets the *Rosaldo* in the harbor of Port Sudan on April 27th.

The First Undersea Village

The Italian freighter, just slightly bigger than *Calypso,* had left Nice on April 10th with the various prefabricated components necessary to construct the "village" to be submerged at Shab

Conshelf II on Shab Rumi in the Red Sea. Moored at great depth, her stern tied to the coral reef, Calypso *provides food and equipment for the underwater village.*

Rumi. She is also carrying other indispensable equipment—compressors, generators, and a large recompression chamber in case of diving accidents. She also had on board most of the personnel who are to take part in the expedition—among others, Jacques Chouteau, professor of physiology.

Alinat, Christian Perrien, and Alexis Sivirine have been in Port Sudan since the 25th. The *Rosaldo* will soon be permanently anchored inside the lagoon of Shab Rumi. Once the *Rosaldo* is safely moved, *Calypso* will make fifteen shuttles during

On the coral reef, Maurice Léandri, Bonnici, Robino, and Sivirine are building the 100-foot-long bridge between Calypso and Rosaldo, anchored inside the lagoon of Shab Rumi.

The diving saucer leaves the garage with her lights on, accompanied by a diver armed against sharks. She is going to descend along the cliff of the coral reef.

Under the keel of Calypso, the village under the sea: the big house, the garage for the saucer, and the fishpond.

the month between Port Sudan and Shab Rumi, a distance of 27 miles each way, to prepare her own anchorages, transport the equipment, and finally, tow out to the site the structures assembled in Port Sudan. To submerge the two main houses and the garage, more than a hundred tons of lead pigs weighing 110 pounds each have to handled and positioned underwater by *Calypso's* divers. On June 12th, the oceanauts—Professor Vaissières, Claude Wesley, Pierre Vanoni, Albert Falco, and Pierre Guilbert—take possession of the "starfish house" at 33 feet. Canoë Kientzy and André Portelatine enter their "little house" at 83 feet on July 5th.

The surface control room has been installed on the *Rosaldo*. During 30 days, the oceanauts worked hard under medical control. They carried out biological experiments in their undersea laboratory, were exposed to sun lamps daily, relaxed by playing chess and listening to music. Guilbert, the cook, tamed a large triggerfish. A parrot was their noisy pet. During one week, the deeper oceanauts safely made much deeper dives than anticipated, reaching several times 330 feet, but they suffered from excessive moisture. Vanoni, who on land suffered from claustrophobia, did not feel uncomfortable at any time. Among the visitors who came all the way to witness Conshelf II were Dr. Charles Aquadro from the U.S. Navy and Cousteau's son Philippe, then twenty-two years old.

The oceanauts return safely to the surface on July 14th, the French national day. The dismantling operations begin. Once again, *Calypso* shut-tles back and forth between Shab Rumi and Port Sudan. The saucer garage is left behind.

On July 25th *Calypso* and the *Rosaldo* leave Port Sudan together and are welcomed back in Marseille on August 15th. The film *World Without Sun* is awarded Cousteau's second Oscar.

"Everyday" Oceanography

After a ten-day rest, *Calypso* resumes scientific activities that are felt almost like routine after the Red Sea adventure.

—at the end of August, saucer dives in the canyon of Cassidaigne near Canis to examine the site selected for a project of dumping "red mud" (the wastes from an aluminum factory at Gardame) through a 3-mile-long undersea pipeline

—in September a trip to the island of Alborán where Cousteau wants to film again the deep kelp forest that he has already explored

—in October a hydrology program for Professor Lacombe in the Nice-Corsica region using the RANA navigation system

—from November 5th to November 11th, a program of biology between Cassis and Saint-Tropez for Professor Vaissières to study the deep benthos populations

—from November 12th to November 20th, saucer dives in the vicinity of Port-Vendres

—finally, to end the year, *Calypso's* team completes a geological program and a study of radioactivity.

Familiar scene at the end of a mission: two troikas, the saucer, and antishark cages are unloaded on the dock.

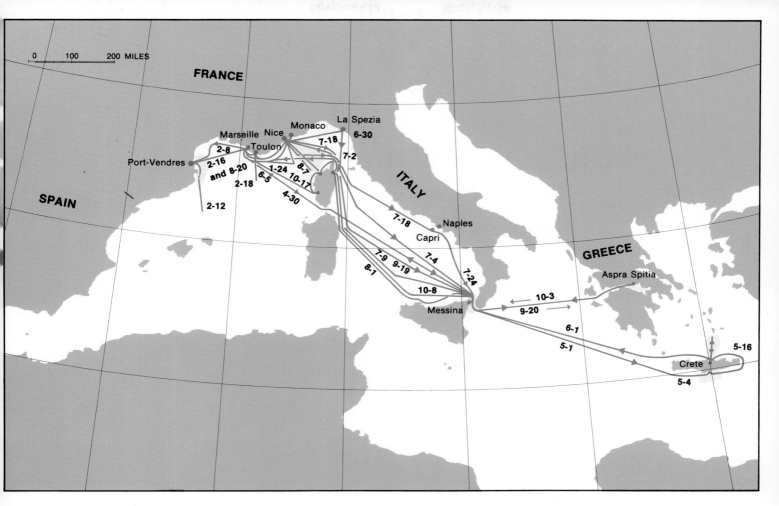

1964

"The Mysterious Island"

A Laboratory-Buoy

Calypso's schedule for 1964 is so heavy that the repairs traditionally made during the month of January are limited to those considered absolutely necessary.

Her first task consists of taking part in towing and anchoring the new laboratory-buoy, nicknamed the "Mysterious Island," conceived by Captain Alinat and developed by the OFRS team in Monaco under the supervision of the engineer, J. Picard.

The laboratory-buoy, constructed on the principle of Froude's pole, is 200 feet long and floats vertically in the water, permitting permanent research at sea in a given location and under stable, efficient conditions practically unaffected by the worst sea conditions. The need for such perfectly stable platforms was simultaneously and independently felt by the Cousteau team and by the Scripps Institute of Oceanography, in La Jolla, California. The latter developed "Flip," an even

The laboratory-buoy, a 200-foot-long Froude pole, in the bay of Villefranche-sur-mer. It is going to be towed and anchored midway between Nice and Corsica.

larger structure, towed horizontally and "flipped" in a vertical position on the site of operation. But "Flip" was a drifting lab, while "Mysterious Island" was to be anchored.

The buoy is in the harbor at Villefranche-sur-mer. *Calypso* makes her way there on January 20th to transfer 2,210 gallons of fuel and 2,080 gallons of water into the buoy's storage tanks. A navy ship, the *Marcel Le Bihan*, carries the heavy moorings, a thick nylon and dacron braided anchor line two miles long and, on January 21st, begins the towing of "Mysterious Island" at a very slow speed. It takes four days for both ships to reach the anchoring spot, located halfway between Nice and Corsica. All maneuvers take place without difficulty and the floating island is delivered to the scientists who are to work aboard it for ten years. Then *Calypso* undertakes less spectacular assignments:

—drillings and corings to identify the targets indicated by Edgerton's mud penetrator off Cap-d'Ail
—a hydrology program with Professor Lacombe between Marseille and Port-Vendres
—current and wind measurements in the Nice-Corsica region
—an inspection of the red mud dumpings at Cassis, with Professor Dangeard.

On March 17th, all programs are halted for a major overhaul.

On April 18th, saucer dives are resumed with Dr. Pérès' biological team in Crete, and for the first time, a pilot other than Albert Falco, Kientzy, nicknamed Canoë, a diver with *Calypso* for ten years, takes the scientists down.

From June 2d to June 26th, a seismic-reflection program begins in the Western Mediterranean. It involves testing new equipment—sparkers, boomers, air guns—and is interrupted to take André Maréchal, then head of the French national scientific research program, to visit the facilities of the laboratory-buoy. Reporters and television crews are on hand.

A Submersible Chamber for Deep Dives

On June 29th, *Calypso* leaves for La Spezia to take delivery of a Galeazzi SDC (submersible decompression chamber), an indispensable tool for deep diving. From La Spezia, *Calypso* sails to Messina to carry out a detailed geophysical and geological survey in the Strait in connection with the Italian project of building a high bridge from Sicily to mainland Italy.

On July 15th, Professor Ivanoff's optical studies once again take *Calypso* to Messina, Palermo, and the area around the Stromboli volcano.

On August 4th, another seismic-refraction program to determine the subsoil structures between the mainland and Corsica.

On August 19th, *Calypso* returns to Port-Vendres for saucer dives in the nearby deep canyons.

On September 13, once again *Calypso* checks the effects of potential red mud dumping. This time in Greece, at Aspra Spitia in the Gulf of Corinth.

From October 1st to the 10th, *Calypso* returns to the Strait of Messina for more detailed studies in connection with Sicily bridge project.

The last months of the year are devoted to perfecting deep-diving methods in preparation for operation "Conshelf III."

A series of training dives to depths running from 260 to 330 feet is initiated from *Calypso* using the Galeazzi chamber and a helium-oxygen mixture. Two teams of six oceanauts are trained off Villefranche under the supervision of Captain Cousteau, Captain Alinat, Dr. Charles Aquadro, Professor Chouteau, and Dr. Xavier Fructus.

Accustomed to suffering from "rapture of the deep"—often named nitrogen narcosis—at depths beyond 150 feet, the divers are delighted to find that they keep a clear mind when breathing heliox. It is a revelation for them, but Falco remarks with some disappointment: "On air, we find everything so beautiful, but with heliox, the reality is there, gray and sad." Surfacing, however, is a long and tedious operation.

By December 15th, hundreds of dives have been made and *Calypso* can return to Marseille for maintenance and major repairs.

The Galeazzi submersible decompression chamber (SDC) will allow deep dives with gas mixtures.

In front of the control panel of the gas mixtures, Cousteau and Alinat talk with Bonnici, one of the divers.

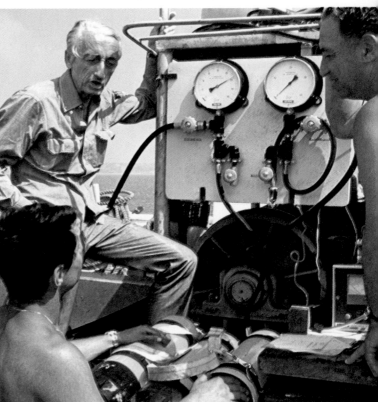

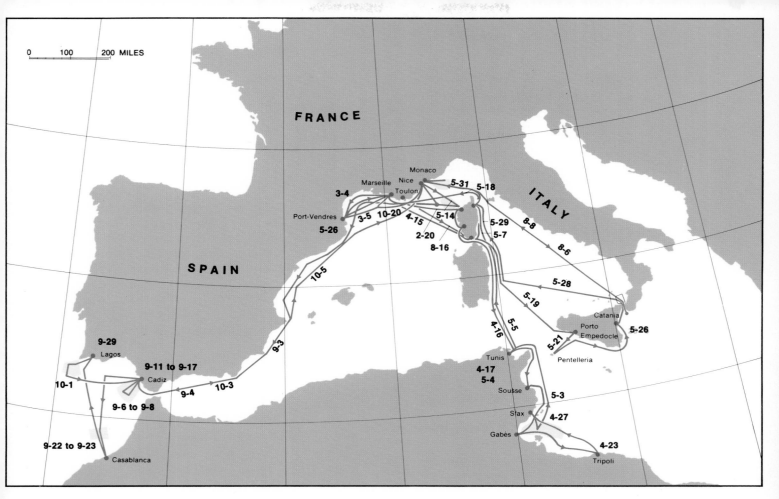

Fire on the High Seas

Another tragedy mobilizes *Calypso's* entire team in Marseille on February 20, 1965; an SOS message is received on board: the laboratory-buoy is on fire. It is 7 P.M. Mollard, Laban, and Plé leave for the city to muster their comrades. In the meantime, *Calypso* prepares to sail as soon as Captain Cousteau, who is flying in from Paris in a private jet, reaches the ship. *Calypso* makes for the buoy at top speed when she receives word from the maritime police in Toulon at 7:40 A.M. that the buoy's six passengers have been rescued by the *Alizée,* a small freighter. *Calypso* reaches the buoy at 11:30 A.M. and Captain Cousteau finds that all that remains of the buoy's upper works is an empty, burned-out shell. A few hours were all it took to reduce the first floating marine laboratory to nothing. The buoy had seemed almost perfect and within the space of thirteen months, had carried out twenty-one successive scientific programs.

Calypso arrives in Nice at 1 P.M. Captain Cousteau starts an investigation. The buoy's occupants, François Varlet, Pierre Oriol, J.P. Rebert, J.P. Bassaget, and C. Wesly, led by the skipper of the buoy, Gabriel Mariani, had made their escape in an inflatable dinghy in the middle of the night. They had to jump 60 feet into the black water to reach the dinghy.

Calypso returns to Marseille. The buoy will be reconstructed and will serve for eight more years.

The Most Varied Programs

The originality of *Calypso's* work is to dedicate the efforts of her team as well as to standard oceanographic surveys as to the most daring pioneering experiments. The diversity of her scientific tasks was highlighted in 1965 by the Conshelf III experiment.

The laboratory-buoy being set up near Nice.

The first program of the year is routine hydrology, from February 26th to March 16th with Professor Lacombe's team around the mouth of the Rhone and off the coast of Nice, using a new air-sea buoy.

From March 22nd to April 6th, *Calypso* is off on a geophysical and acoustical program with Professor Muraour off the southern coast of France, using hydrophones near the surface and geophones on the bottom.

From April 13th to May 10th, *Calypso* is away to Tunisia and Libya for a biological and geological survey led by J. Picard. The program involves photographic profiles with the troika and hydrology studies, as well as corings and soundings, bottom dredgings, and plankton hauls.

From May 12th to May 31st, an undersea optical program for Professor Ivanoff is carried out from Nice to Ile du Levant, Corsica, Sicily, the island of Pantelleria, Catania in Sicily, Bastia, and then back to Nice again.

Other investigations, of course, are also accomplished just as they are every year, with the saucer and the troika under the direction of Professor Vaissières. They take place off the coasts of Marseille and Corsica.

From June 20th to the 26th: dredgings, samplings and saucer dives in the area of Cape Bear and Port-Vendres with Professor Louis Glangeaud.

In July, August, October, November, and December, five periods of two weeks are devoted to an accurate mapping of the entire zone covered by the RANA radionavigation system, from Italy to Toulon and most of Corsica. The sounding profiles are followed along a very tight grid and will be used to print the most detailed topographic charts of the area.

Various requests for CNRS are also honored:

—a study of deep currents in the Cadiz-Casablanca area; seawater radioactivity measurements in the Western Mediterranean; a number of trips, using Monaco's seismic profiling equipment; diving with the saucer near Nice and Marseille.

Allo! Aquanauts! Oceanauts Speaking

As the U.S. Navy is carrying out project Sealab 2 at a depth of 200 feet off San Diego in the Pacific, the *Calypso* team is busy conducting experiment Conshelf III 328 feet down, off Cape Ferret near Villefranche. Conshelf III is a spherical structure, 20 feet in diameter, equipped to accommodate in safety and comfort six oceanauts, Christian Bownia, Raymond Coll, Yves Omer, Philippe Cousteau, André Laban, and Jacques Rollet, during their 27 days at 328 feet below sea level. The deep divers enter the sphere in the harbor of Monaco. They are progressively submitted to a pressure of eleven atmospheres in a mixture of oxygen and helium. The sphere is then towed to Cape Ferret by *Calypso* escorted by the *Espadon;* it is slowly submerged to the selected site and is connected by power and communication cables to the Cape Ferret lighthouse. The medical, physical, and physiological data taken inside by Rollet are fed into a powerful computer on shore. Daily, the oceanauts swim out and perform heavy and difficult duties for two hours at a depth of 394 feet on a symbolic oil wellhead installed there by *Calypso*. Philippe takes photographs and films. One evening, a telephone conversation is established between Conshelf III and Sealab 2. In their Donald Duck voice distorted by helium, oceanaut Philippe exchanges greetings and good wishes with astronaut-aquanaut Scott Carpenter from the bottom of the Mediterranean to the bottom of the Pacific. The deep divers, at the end of the experiment, are towed back under pressure to Monaco and safely decompressed during three days in the harbor.

The cost of the operation is disproportionate to available resources and *Calypso*'s team remains in debt several years. But a one hour "special" is made for American television with the financial help of the National Geographic Society, which will have a profound influence on *Calypso*'s destiny.

All in all, 1965 is a very full year indeed for *Calypso*. On December 18th, she returns to Marseille, where Vincent Bianco awaits her for extensive repairs.

From Cap Ferrat to Monaco Calypso tows Conshelf III, where six men will spend 27 days at a depth beyond 330 feet.

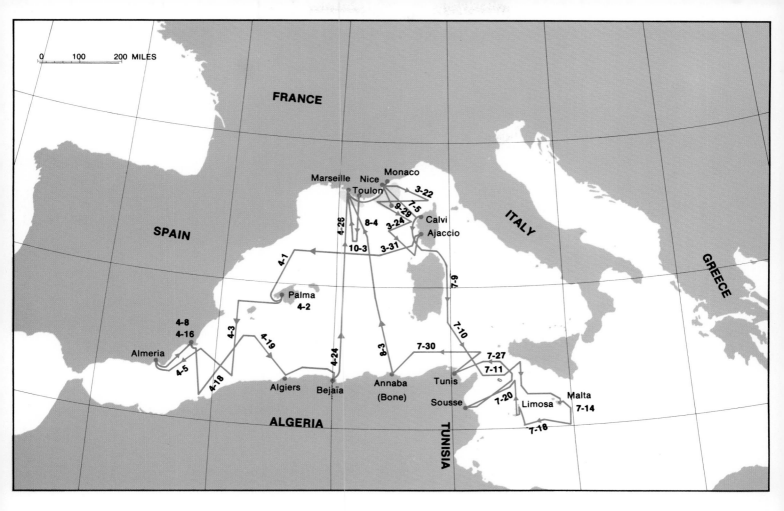

1966

The Year of the Great Careening

Although *Calypso* is dry-docked twice a year and carefully overhauled every year, usually in the wintertime, complete remodelings have been rare. The last one goes back to 1957. Cousteau decides that 1966 is the year for another refitting. The work, however, is to be carried out in two stages, the first one in January and the second one stretched out over October, November, and December.

From February 25th to April 20th, *Calypso* carries out a series of geological studies of structures occurring at great depths which appear to be related to "salt mounds." They were first discovered by *Calypso* as far back as 1957. To this end, improved seismic-reflection equipment is set up in the Nice-Corsica region.

A more extensive seismic operation involving two ships, *Calypso* and the *Jean Charcot*, a new French oceanographic vessel, covers the entire Western Mediterranean basin, from Nice to Corsica, Sardinia, Majorca, the Spanish and Algerian coasts. At Cassis, *Calypso* supervises the laying

Completely remodeled and equipped with new features that make her more functional, Calypso arrives in Monaco, passing the Museum of Oceanography of which Cousteau is director.

November 26, 1966, the new deckhouse is hoisted on board.

of a controversial underwater pipeline, which is to deposit in deep water the famous red mud from an aluminum factory.

On a Sunken Airplane

No sooner has this work been completed than representatives from a foreign airline company ask *Calypso* to quickly locate and bring to the surface the wreck of a DeHavilland, an airplane that had just crashed and sunk in 650 to 950 feet of water not far from the airport in Nice. The plane is located the first day, but as the diving saucer descends it triggers an avalanche of mud, partially burying the wreckage. It takes two weeks of hard work to dig out and examine the wreckage. Several important pieces are recovered with the help of a grapnel towed by the saucer.

From July 4th to August 4, with Professor Ivanoff, several new devices record optical properties of seawater along a route which follows Corsica, the Corsican-Tunisian Shelf, Malta, Sousse, Tunis, Bejaïa, and Marseille.

Still other programs: from August 9th to August 17th, Dangeard, professor of geology, uses the diving saucer and the troika; from August 20 to September 30th, Professor Pérès dives in the saucer, south of Toulon; from August 20th to September 30th, a seismic trip to record the effects at sea of explosions set off in the Lac Nègre by the International Geophysical Association.

On September 12th, the saucer dives with Gaston Deferre, the mayor of Marseille, at the famous site of Cassidaigne and the red mud.

Once again, *Calypso* carries out a campaign of radioactivity measurements in seawater at a depth of 1,000 feet.

Finally, a seismic-reflection program monitored by troika is carried out from October 1st to the 11th.

A Face Lift for a New Life

The year 1966 marks a new orientation in *Calypso*'s activities. For the past fifteen years she has been the only French oceanographic vessel in existence; researchers and scientific institutions have competed for her services. But this year a brand new oceanographic vessel, the *Jean Charcot*, puts out to sea, and *Calypso* is freed for other tasks. Moreover, the film shot during the Conshelf III experiment is an enormous success on American television; it leads to a contract for a series of twelve more films, which provides financial backing for the ship for three years. A major remodeling can thus be initiated.

The ship is stripped. The barges are sandblasted, the furniture is repaired; the main electric battery is removed for good and is replaced by transformers to switch the ship to shore lines when in a harbor. The smokestack is taken down to be completely redone. The deckhouse is entirely rearranged and the crew's quarters are rebuilt with separate cabins accommodating two persons. Electric motors, mufflers, and rudders are all taken to the shipyards to be overhauled. The winch is removed to be rebuilt with two separate drums. The davits are removed and reconstructed to support a weight of one and a half tons, and a 25 kw. rotary converter is added to energize all our new precision instruments. The propulsion

engines and the generators are completely redone, and a new pilothouse is put in place on November 26th. The "false nose" is replaced with a newer model that has a larger observation chamber with better visibility.

The ship is floated on December 28th. The only thing left to do is equip the quarterdeck to handle additional equipment—a Galeazzi chamber for deep dives, and our two new one-man minisubs, type P500, nicknamed "Sea Fleas."

The new look of the forecastle.

January 1967—September 1970

Yves Omer and Owen Lee with the underwater movie cameras.

The Great Expedition

Before he leaves on a three-year trip, Captain Cousteau invites Prince Rainier and Princess Grace of Monaco to a farewell reception.

By the end of Janury, the ship is ready and moored in Monaco. During a press conference aboard ship on February 18th, Captain Cousteau unfolds to journalists the three-year program during which the first twelve films of the television series called "The Undersea World of Jacques Cousteau" will be shot. Cousteau emphasizes the destruction already made in the world's oceans by pollution or overfishing. He feels compelled to record on color film for future generations the vanishing marvels of the silent world. A farewell reception is held at the end of the press conference and is attended by Their Serene Highnesses Prince Rainier and Princess Grace of Monaco. After many hands have been shaken and hundreds of balloons have been released, *Calypso* sails for the Red Sea. She will not return to Europe until almost four years later, upon completion of her longest expedition.

Despite the pain of two broken vertebrae suffered in a recent automobile accident, Captain Cousteau is aboard ship with Mrs. Cousteau. Frédéric Dumas, one of the Captain's oldest friends and a fellow-diver from the beginning, is also taking part in the voyage. And we mustn't forget the new mascot aboard ship—an imposing bloodhound christened Zoom, presented to Mrs. Cousteau by Her Serene Highness Princess Grace as the ship left.

Calypso has taken on a considerable amount of equipment: the diving saucer S.P. 350; the Galaezzi chamber for deep dives using helium-oxygen mixtures; 15 underwater cameras conceived and built by Cousteau's specialists at OFRS; and new streamlined aqualungs to increase the divers' speed. These sophisticated devices include built-in radio and sonar telephones, a searchlight in the helmet, an emergency buzzer and an anti-shark billy. Together with new suits, the super aqualungs gave the divers a stylish appearance that was to become popular on television. *Calypso* divers are also "motorized" by undersea scooters.

In the past fifteen years, the *Calypso* team acquired a serious oceanographic background by closely cooperating with top scientists of various disciplines. Now comes the time to use all this experience for worldwide exploration, careful observation, and filming of the behavior of marine animals, and to inform the public at large of the dangers that threaten the oceans.

The expedition is to be documented by the researchers and scientists of the Oceanographic Museum of Monaco, of which Captain Cousteau is director since 1957. For each of the films, *Calypso* will carry an undisputed international expert in the field to supervise the accuracy of the work.

Once in the Red Sea, *Calypso* meets the *Espadon*, the 57-foot tender that has paved the way for *Calypso* for several months. Albert Falco and Philippe Cousteau are aboard and have already located the most favorable underwater sites. From the beginning of March on, the dives follow one another, in Shakar Zeberjëid, Suakin, and Djebel Teir. The ship sails out of the Red Sea, passes by Djibouti and reaches the island of Socotra on March 13th.

In the Land of 1,000 Atolls

On the way to the Maldives Islands, the ship runs into a pod of sperm whales and encounters two days of bad weather. Then on March 8th, at two o'clock in the morning, there is a loud crack and an engine begins to race. The shaft of the starboard propeller has just broken again. *Calypso* is brought to a standstill at a distance of 1,800 miles from all major ports.

With the help of Bonnici and Coll, Falco dives and manages—in the middle of the night—to secure the shaft and propeller so that they will not damage the rudder. *Calypso* then makes her way towards the Maldives at seven knots on a single engine. The two nearest shipyards are Colombo to the east and Mombasa to the west. Cousteau decides to continue the expedition.

The ship arrives in the Lari Atoll on March 21st and the team goes to work. During the exciting weeks that follow, they explore and film the coral and underwater life of these islands where the inhabitants live in houses made from blocks of coral. They observe strange old friends they had discovered in Madeira in 1948: the "garden eels" that live buried in the mud and emerge from it curved like question marks.

On April 7th, *Calypso* leaves the Maldives for the Seychelles and arrives at Mahé on April 18th.

On April 24th, *Calypso* visits Cosmoledo Island, north of Madagascar—still a wild paradise—and Assumption Island. She then steers towards Pemba Island, near Zanzibar, on the 29th, still running on only one engine.

On May 5th, *Calypso* is at Mombasa. The monsoon season is approaching. Fortunately the spare propeller shaft has arrived. *Calypso* is repaired and sails from Mombasa at normal speed.

En route, the alarm bell sounds. A black mass, 45 feet long, appears portside. A Zodiac is lowered into the water with Falco, Barsky, Deloire, and Coll. The mass turns out to be an inoffensive but enormous whale shark. Deloire succeeds in filming it head on, while Coll manages to cling to the

After being apart for a few months, Calypso *and* Espadon *meet again in the Red Sea.*

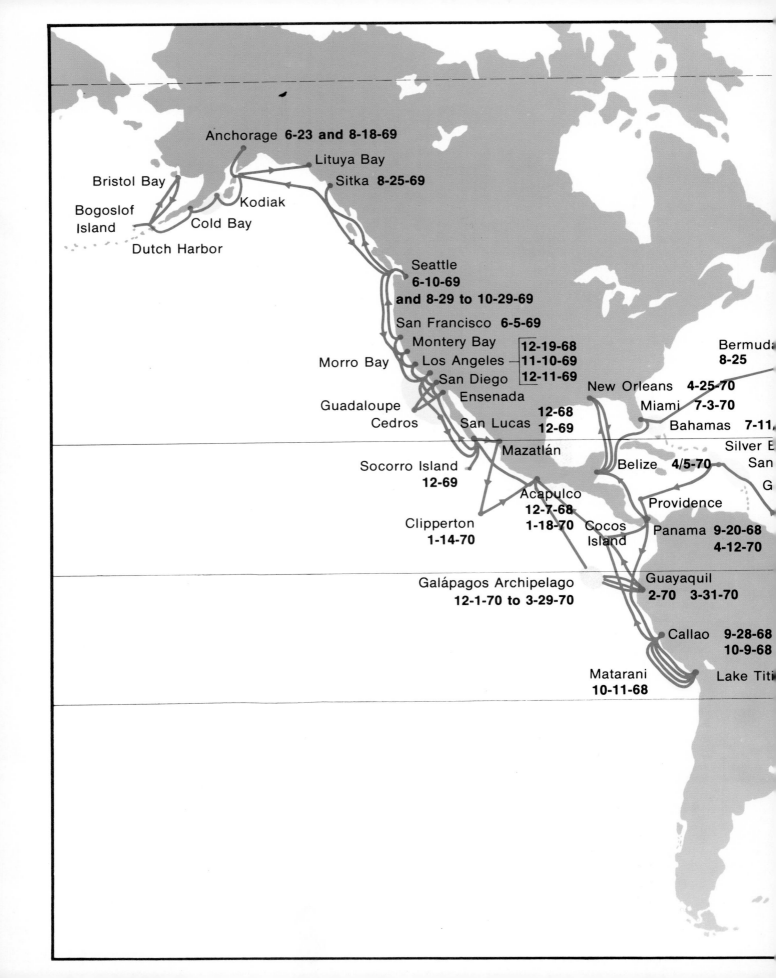

Anchorage **6-23 and 8-18-69**

Bristol Bay

Lituya Bay

Sitka **8-25-69**

Bogoslof
Island

Kodiak

Cold Bay

Dutch Harbor

Seattle
6-10-69
and 8-29 to 10-29-69

San Francisco **6-5-69**

Montery Bay

Morro Bay

Los Angeles — | **12-19-68** |
| **11-10-69** |
| **12-11-69** |

San Diego

Ensenada

Guadaloupe

Cedros

San Lucas

12-68

12-69

Mazatlán

Bermuda
8-25

New Orleans **4-25-70**

Miami **7-3-70**

Bahamas **7-11**

Silver E

San

Socorro Island
12-69

Belize **4/5-70**

G

Acapulco
12-7-68
1-18-70

Providence

Clipperton
1-14-70

Cocos
Island

Panama **9-20-68**
4-12-70

Galápagos Archipelago
12-1-70 to 3-29-70

Guayaquil
2-70   3-31-70

Callao   **9-28-68**
10-9-68

Matarani
10-11-68

Lake Titi

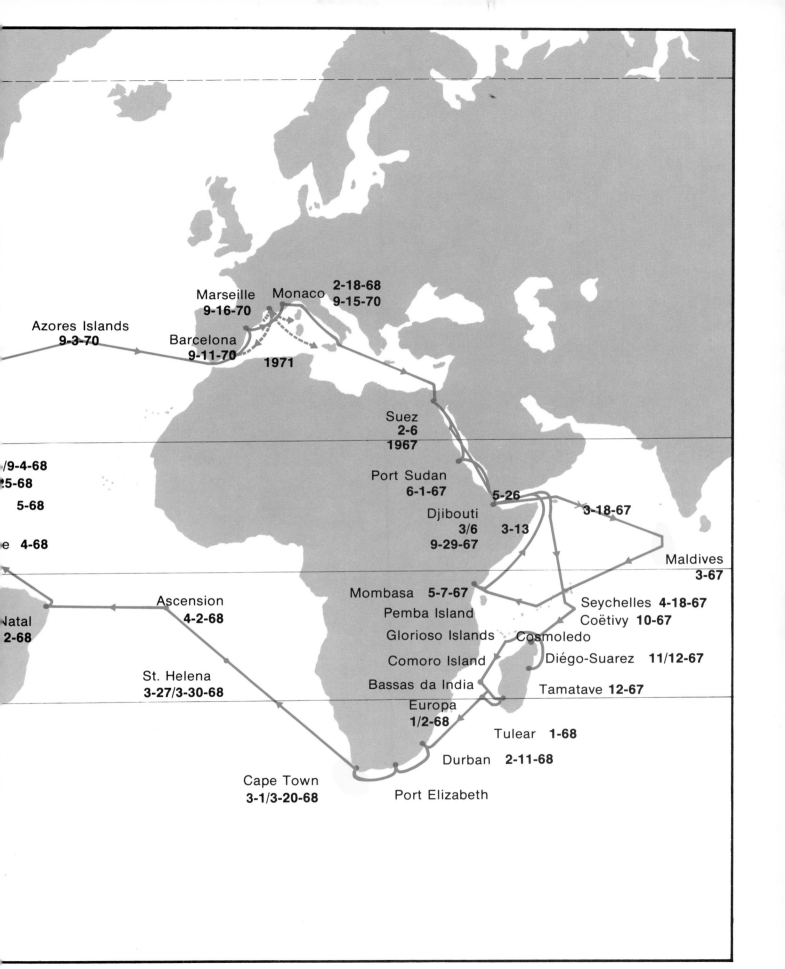

Azores Islands
9-3-70

Marseille
9-16-70

Monaco **2-18-68**
9-15-70

Barcelona
9-11-70

1971

Suez
2-6
1967

Port Sudan
6-1-67

5-26

Djibouti
3/6   **3-13**
9-29-67

3-18-67

Maldives
3-67

Mombasa   **5-7-67**

Pemba Island

Glorioso Islands

Comoro Island

Bassas da India

Seychelles   **4-18-67**

Coëtivy   **10-67**

Cosmoledo

Diégo-Suarez   **11/12-67**

Tamatave   **12-67**

/9-4-68

:5-68

5-68

e **4-68**

Ascension
4-2-68

St. Helena
3-27/3-30-68

Natal
2-68

Europa
1/2-68

Tulear   **1-68**

Durban   **2-11-68**

Cape Town
3-1/3-20-68

Port Elizabeth

Launching one of the monoseat diving saucers nicknamed "Sea Fleas 500." The second saucer is on the hold panel.

dorsal fin. Another whale shark appears, this one even larger—maybe 50 feet long—and the team films it in turn.

The following day, *Calypso* stops in the vicinity of the coastal reefs to mark sharks so their migrations can be studied.

Calypso calls at Djibouti on the 25th. She crosses the Strait of Bab el Mandeb in a sandstorm and finally finds herself in the Red Sea, sheltered from the monsoon. Sharks are extensively studied and filmed around the spectacular coral reefs of the Red Sea. *Calypso* arrives in Port Sudan on June 1st. The *Espadon* is there to greet her.

Trapped!

On June 3d, the entire team pays a visit to Shab Rumi, where the saucer garage of the Conshelf II undersea village was left behind 35 feet down in 1963. A few patches of coral have already grown on the roof. *Calypso* is warned by radio that relations between Egypt and Israel are growing more and more tense. War is imminent. Cousteau decides to return to France at all costs, and after considerable difficulties, he succeeds.

War is declared. *Calypso* and the *Espadon* arrive in Suez . . . and there they are trapped. As the ships lie anchored side by side in the harbor, bombs are dropped around the ships, nearby oil tanks are set in flames and all the equipment in crates that had been unloaded on the dock is machine-gunned by Israeli planes.

On July 21st, hostilities cease. A complete new team led by Captain Bougaran arrives to relay the Maritano team. Albert Falco is replaced by Raymond Kientzy (Canoë) as head diver.

The Suez Canal is closed for many years to come. *Calypso* improvises perforce an Indian Ocean program. The *Espadon* is left behind; *Calypso*'s little sister will round the Cape of Good Hope and sail back to Europe . . . but safely, on the deck of a German freighter.

A Hot-Air Balloon

On her southern route to Djibouti along the Red Sea, *Calypso* logs hundreds of dives and piles up miles of film.

Several sunken ships are discovered and a detailed map is made of Shab Arab, a coral reef 30 miles

A diver waits at decompression level, using the hull of Calypso *to avoid reaching the surface too soon.*

One of the "Sea Fleas" being released from the crane.

east of Djibouti. From Djibouti army helicopters bring divers and their equipment over barren chaotic landscapes to Lake Assal. The lake is so salty that even with a ballast of 66 pounds the divers barely manage to descend. The bottom of the lake is completely covered by salt crystals which sometimes take on the shapes of flowers. The challenging experience results in a cruel irritation of the divers' skin . . . and some unusual film.

On September 22d, off Djibouti, a hot-air balloon is tested by Philippe Cousteau; in need of an airborne filming platform, his idea is to try an inexpensive substitute for a helicopter, which *Calypso* is not yet equipped to accommodate.

The balloon is filled with hot air and Philippe steps in the gondola. He takes off, picks up altitude, descends, lands in the water—up to his safety belt—and then ascends again at the very last minute! Several tries are required to bring the temperamental device under control.

Calypso leaves Djibouti in very good weather. She films pods of sperm whales in the Gulf of Oman and studies their behavior. Several experiments reveal both the superior intelligence of these huge mammals, and their fatal slowness to react at the first approach of ships.

The Minisubs

Once again *Calypso* travels south in the Indian Ocean. At the end of October she reaches the island of Coëtivy near the Seychelles, where brightly colored groupers are plentiful. A crowd of sick people file aboard to be examined by Dr. Millet, the ship's doctor, happy to be back on the job after having been frustrated by a healthy crew for some four years.

On November 9th, the ship docks at Diégo-Suarez in Madagascar for careening and maintenance before spending weeks of unforgettable dives around the Glorious Islands.

The minisubs arrive in Tamatave, Madagascar, by freighter. They are embarked as a crowd of curious, unbelieving Malagasy look on. The twin minisubs weigh about two tons each and are powered by jets like the diving saucer S.P. 350, from which they were developed. The one-man devices are light and maneuverable and will introduce the "buddy system" dives in the behavior of exploration submersibles. They can film each other, work with each other, and eventually come to each other's rescue.

At the end of the year, a second "change of the guard": the Bourgaran team is relieved by the Maritano team. On New Year's Eve, following a tradition of the ship, the crew makes a dive at night on Leven's Bank.

Typhoons Just Like Those in Joseph Conrad

On January 1st, *Calypso* calls again at the Glorious Islands and then reaches north to the Comoro Islands, where an obstinate search for the famous living fossil fish, the coelacanth, is carried out–in vain. Much further south, she explores one of the rare Indian Ocean atolls to be covered by a few feet of water: Bassas da India. Finally, she arrives at the island of Europa on January 9th.

Like many coral islands, Europa has an underwater channel between 345 and 360 feet deep, where sea level was during a late glacial period. The team uses the equipment it has for deep dives to explore the grottos that cut through the cliffs above the channel.

The level of the sea has gone up and down according to glaciation periods, and whenever it remained stable for a few millennia, it left scars on the submerged cliffs of the reef all around the world.

At 150 feet, "fossil beaches" are found, with nearby caves—in Europa, *Calypso's* divers explore such deep caves the Galeazzi chamber is submerged to a depth of 82 feet, to serve as a decompression chamber. Falco, Coll, and Deloire are breathing a mixture of 50 percent air and 50 percent helium. They are excited by the enchanting sights in the grotto, but for every ten minutes spent at 360 feet, they have to undergo two hours of decompression in the chamber.

The sky darkens, the sea turns rough, and the local meteorological station announces that two typhoons, named "Flossie" and "Georgette," are on their way. "Flossie" passes near Europa and forces *Calypso* to move away from the island to protect herself at sea, leaving behind a team of cameramen; their camp is destroyed by rainstorms and winds reaching 160 knots.

On January 23d, the ship painstakingly retrieves the exhausted team from the island in spite of a violent storm. Then she sails for Tulear to take shelter from the second typhoon, but once again, the starboard propeller shaft breaks. In the open sea, with waves 10 feet high and a 55 knot wind, Raymond Coll, Christian Bonnici, and Bernard Chauvelin work for two hours to move the shaft forward and free the rudder. This accomplished, *Calypso* heads for Tulear at a speed of 6 knots, fleeing the cyclone that grows wilder behind her. At Tulear, she experiences the full fury of "Georgette." The storm is moving at more than 80 miles an hour, and as it passes over Africa twenty-three lives are lost.

Returning to France via the Suez Canal is out of the question. *Calypso* has no choice but to sail round the Cape of Good Hope; she will cross the Atlantic on her way to the Caribbean.

The First of the Three Capes

Sailors (it is said) only have the right to spit in the wind if they've rounded the three capes: Good Hope, Horn, and the cape south of Tasmania. *Calypso* is about to tackle the first.

Calypso arrives in Durban on February 11th, where the broken propeller shaft is replaced. After putting in at Saint Croix Island and Ile aux Oiseaux, the home of colonies of penguins, she calls at Port Elizabeth and heads for the Cape, where she will work from March 1st to the 20th. Many dives are made around the Cape in forests of giant kelp swinging in the large swell. Two sea

Near Europa Island, the sea is so rough that Calypso *has to take refuge in Tulear.*

En route under the sky of the Cape of Good Hope.

At Matarani, the minisubs and their equipment are loaded onto the train that will take them to Lake Titicaca.

A platform is set on the bow to make the search for whales easier.

lions, Pepito and Cristobal, are captured. They are provided with a home and a swimming pool and share *Calypso*'s life for seven months . . . the sea lions familiarize themselves with the team to the point of becoming diving companions and returning on board of their free will—an extraordinary experience in communal living, shared by men and marine mammals within the narrow confines of a boat.

Calypso stops twice during her fifth Atlantic crossing, at Saint Helena Island, where Napoleon was exiled, and at Ascension Island. All the way from Capetown to Natal, Brazil, *Calypso* measures the amount of micrometeorites, the dust that falls from outer space and may be a factor of the amount of life produced by the sea.

Calypso calls at Cayenne, where François Varlet, a physical oceanographer, embarks, and arrives at Puerto Rico on April 25th. Commander Caillart replaces Captain Maritano. Most of the free dives with the sea lions are made in May and June in the Caribbean, at Gaudeloupe, Saint Barthélemy, the Barbados, Saint Thomas, and San Juan.

Treasure Hunt!

Calypso docks in Puerto Rico June 22d, 23d and 24th and sails to the Silver Bank, a coral reef at water level as big as a French province. The approach to the reefs is very dangerous—ever since the sixteenth century, ships that have encountered it have broken up, spilling their often precious cargo over coral gardens.

By following the directions of Remy de Haenen, adventurer and mayor of the small island of Saint Barthélemy, *Calypso*'s team hopes to find the hulk of a famous Spanish galleon, the *Nuestra Señora de la Concepción*, known to be carrying a fabulous treasure stolen from the New World. The wreckage of a large wooden ship is indeed located. From July 15th to September 4th, amid hellish heat and with food and water supplies running low, the team exhausts itself handling the temperamental air lift, breaking up tons of coral with a sledgehammer and fishing out rusted cannon balls and broken crockery. The sunken ship is not the *Nuestra Señora de la Concepción* after all, but a merchant vessel that sailed sometime after 1756. And there is no treasure!

After taking supplies in San Juan, *Calypso* sails for Cristobal (at the entrance to the Panama Canal), passing off the coast of Nicaragua and the Saint André Islands where the minisubs make two dives. The canal is crossed on September 20th—*Calypso* is in the Pacific. She drops anchor at Foca Island to film pelicans, sharks, dolphins, and swordfish. She then steers due south towards Peru, where Jean-Michel Cousteau has been in charge of preparing a difficult expedition to the Andes.

The Lake of Toads

At Matarani, *Calypso* draws up to the wharf and transfers onto a special train an enormous amount of equipment: the two minisubs, a decompression chamber, a compressor, aqualungs, cameras. . .

On October 4th, the little train, made especially picturesque by the yellow shapes of the subs, leaves Matarani to slowly climb the Andes mountains. Destination: Lake Titicaca, altitude 12,506 feet. Marcel Ichac, a noted mountain climber and film director, has joined the team. Lake Titicaca had never before been sounded or explored in depth. It is found to be inhabited by millions of toads, that have adapted to underwater life not by developing gills, but by using their skin as membrane to oxygenate their blood. Various artifacts are found.

On November 9th, *Calypso* dry-docks in Callao and while waiting for the group to return from Lake Titicaca, gets under way for hydrology measurements and exploration of the Peruvian coasts.

On November 20th, *Calypso* picks up members of the Lake Titicaca expedition at Matarani. She stocks up on supplies at Callao and then heads towards Acapulco in Mexico on her return trip. Zoom, the bloodhound, is sent back to France with Bernard Delemotte.

The seas are bad. Nevertheless, sperm whales, swordfish, dolphins, sharks, and flying fish escort the ship. *Calypso* calls at Coca Island for a day and arrives in Acapulco on December 7th.

Of Elephant Seals, Whales, and Squid

On the 12th, *Calypso* is in San Lucas, at the southernmost tip of the Baja California Peninsula. André Laban and Canoë dive there with the minisubs.

The ship arrives in Long Beach, near Los Angeles, on December 19th. *Calypso* spends the Christmas holiday there and then sails for Ensenada, near the Mexican border, on the 26th. From there she heads towards the island of Gaudaloupe, the permanent home of colonies of elephant seals. The animals are filmed both on land and in the water. One of the minisubs discovers the natural marine graveyard of these giant seals. *Calypso* returns to San Diego, leaving behind a team of cameramen. They are picked

By the coasts of Colombia.

up on January 8th, 1969, and then the ship sails for Scammon Bay where the gray whales gather to give birth to their young. A film on these "desert whales" and their behavior during reproduction is shot by Philippe Cousteau with the help of Doctor Ted Walker.

Calypso returns to San Diego on January 14th to stock up on provisions and study the problem of the proliferation of sea urchins at Coronado Island.

After a few sorties, mainly to Guadaloupe, a major overhaul is undertaken at the naval shipyard in San Diego from February 10th to March 12th.

On March 21st, *Calypso*'s team is grieved to learn of the death of Captain Cousteau's father, Daniel Cousteau, at the age of ninety-two. Daniel Cousteau had started diving at the age of sixty-seven and had taken a very active part in the administration of *Calypso* during the first ten years of her existence.

From March 25th to June 3d, *Calypso*'s team works on the outskirts of Catalina Island. The ship chases down orcas (the so-called killer whales), groupers, dolphins, and whales daily, either to film them or to measure their speed and diving ability. Off Isthmus Bay, a film is made on the mating orgy of the squid. Some of the schools of frantic squid are so dense they clog up the filters of the ship's pumps.

Those Incredible Machines

An extraordinary jamboree of underwater devices is organized by André Laban. The *Beaver, Dowb, Deep Quest, Nekton, Star II,* and, of course, *Calypso*'s twin minisubs are gathered in Isthmus Bay. Never before have so many exploration submarines been together. They dive as a group and the specialists compare their performances. Then five ships—*Transquest, Search Tide, Dowb Star, Swan,* and *Calypso*—are lined up next to one another so that discussion is easier and a general evaluation can be made.

On June 3d, *Calypso* leaves Long Beach for Morea Bay and then heads north towards San Francisco. She passes beneath the Golden Gate Bridge on June 5th and moors at the wharf.

Visitors and journalists come aboard. She leaves two days later and on June 10th, *Calypso* is in Seattle, the city where she was built. She moors opposite the university. The shipyards where she came into existence twenty-seven years ago no longer exist but engineers and workers who took part in building her come to see the plucky little ship.

Salmon, Otters, and Walruses

On June 27th, the ship sets a course for Alaska. The weather is poor and the sea heavy. On June 19th, *Calypso* is forced to cut speed and take shelter behind Graham Island. She arrives in Anchorage on June 23d.

The new program is to be devoted to sea otters and salmon. On June 25th, *Calypso* is in the Barrens Islands observing and filming sea otters and fur seals. She moors at Kodiak Island and sends out a team in a Zodiac to search for "king crabs," giant spider crabs almost $3\frac{1}{2}$ feet in diameter. Another team led by Falco is put ashore on a "salmon expedition." Jacques Renoir, great grandson of the famous painter, is in charge of photography.

At Cherni Island, on July 9th, the team films and captures some sea otters who are released almost immediately. *Calypso* then sails to Cold Bay to take aboard Captain Cousteau, who is arriving from France. On July 9th, she drops anchor off the island of Unalaska. That same day, at 11:15 A.M., astronauts Armstrong and Aldrin set foot on the moon. Jean-Paul Bassaget, *Calypso*'s captain, notes in his log that Raymond Coll, who at that moment is piloting a minisub at 492 feet, "is the deepest man on earth during the lunar landing." On the quarterdeck, loudspeakers receive simultaneous messages from our barren satellite and from the living bottom of our oceans.

On July 21st, *Calypso* is at Dutch Harbor, then sails towards Round Island, near the northern coast of Bristol Bay. There the team finds the walruses they had been counting on—old males by the hundreds. A team films the animals ashore, while *Calypso* finds herself in front of more than five hundred walruses lying on a beach.

The bad weather persists. *Calypso* backtracks and passes by Amaknak Island and returns to Dutch Harbor where she fills up on fuel and water as well as food.

The ship anchors next off Bogoslof Island. This is the farthest west *Calypso* has ever been. *Calypso* then heads backs towards the Cherni Islands, crossing Akutan Strait once again, and films about fifteen orcas in the channel. There are plenty of otters and they are quite willing film stars. A few of them are temporarily confined in a small bay which the team closes off with nets and the divers have to devote themselves to catching the otters' favourite foods—mussels, sea urchins, and king crabs.

Alaska—many walruses are discovered and filmed on Walrus Island in Bristol Bay.

On the way back, Calypso *stops near the snowy mountains of the Aleutian Islands.*

Calypso puts into port at Kodiak Island to pick up the "salmon team." She then returns to Anchorage for a few days. The engines are serviced and the crew has a chance to relax before crossing the Gulf of Alaska and making their way south to Seattle.

Return to Her Natal Shipyards

In September, *Calypso* is overhauled at the Lake Union Dock in Seattle. There she is visited by an old man with tears in his eyes: he had helped in her construction!

Between the 29th of September and the 29th of October *Calypso* helps shoot a film on giant octupi. The film's heroine is Joan Duffy, a young woman who specializes in the study of these animals. She quietly handles huge octupi larger and almost as heavy as she is.

On October 29th, *Calypso* leaves for Monterey, south of San Francisco. She spends a week there while the film team shoots a cruel sequence: sea otters that capture sunfish and tear their fins off so the fish remain alive but captive.

On November 10th, *Calypso* sails for Long Beach, to be her home port in the United States until December 11th. She makes several trips to the coastal areas around Catalina Island studying dolphins with Professor R.-G. Busnel.

Calypso takes aboard the two minisubs that had been completely overhauled in Seattle and puts out to sea to test them. They are lowered to approximately 2,000 feet. The results are satisfactory.

On December 10th, *Calypso* leaves for Cabo San Lucas. As she skirts Baja California, she runs into a group of 200 to 300 dolphins, a dozen pilot whales and some swordfish. The minisubs dive daily, the cameramen shoot sequences on the barracudas, and a plane arrives to film *Calypso*'s operations.

106

In Mexico, a "Sea Flea" dives at Cape San Lucas.

Christmas at the End of the World

Christmas is celebrated at San Benedicto Island, 250 miles south of Cabo San Lucas, where the minisubs dive in a deep trench to film the sharks that are swimming about. On their return to Cabo San Lucas, the team gathers in *Calypso*'s mess to celebrate the New Year with the traditional midnight supper.

January 1, 1970, everyone is at work at sea, shooting an underwater sequence on the two minisubs as they dive and run through their maneuvers. On January 6th *Calypso* lifts anchor to sail to Mazatlán in Mexico. After she takes on fresh supplies, *Calypso* makes for Clipperton, a typical atoll located 600 miles off the coast of Acapulco, curiously belonging to France. The sharks are numerous in the waters surrounding Clipperton. One of them, measuring $11\frac{1}{2}$ feet in length, leaps out of the water several times. The divers venture into the water only with the protection of the antishark cage. One dive is made in the lagoon and some aerial shots are taken with a helicopter belonging to an American tuna boat.

On January 18th *Calypso* is in Acapulco and on the 25th, sets out for Puerto Angel where the Zodiacs and launches leave to search out manta rays. *Calypso* picks up course again for the Galápagos Islands, arriving on February 1st.

Crossing the equator is celebrated with the traditional ceremony in the greatest gaiety!

The island of Ispana is finally selected as the main site for filming the life of the iguanas and of fur seals. A team is landed there while *Calypso* hurries on to Guayaquil, Ecuador, to take on fresh supplies and change the engine oil. She returns to the Galápagos to furnish the two film crews with fresh provisions and then anchors at the *Bahia* wreck on San Cristóbal Island. It is there that Omer films the behavior of strange creatures called batfish.

While making a study of the potentialities and resources of each island of the Galápagos Archipelago, the divers find very clear deep waters, hammerhead sharks, and enormous manta rays. The team is warmly welcomed by the zoologists at the Darwin Foundation who look after the exceptional fauna on the Galápagos.

In the map chamber of Calypso, *in the Galápagos Archipelago, Dr. Bartholomew gives an EKG to an iguana.*

Tractors are used to tow the ship through the Panama Canal.

Close Call!

The program is thus unfolding without a snag when, on the 27th of March, running at 10 knots between Ispanola and Santa Cruz, *Calypso* hits an underwater rock not shown on the chart. The impact is very violent. The false nose is crushed, the sonar transducer is knocked out of commission, four planks and the garboard are damaged, but the hull holds tight, the propellers are intact and the ship is able to navigate normally.

Calypso calls at Guayaquil on March 31st in response to a request from the Ecuadorian Navy to look for an airplane lost at sea.

Almost as good as new and supplied with fresh provisions, *Calypso* leaves for Coco Island on April 4th. She passes through the Panama Canal on April 12th and is in the Atlantic once again.

Launching of a "Sea Flea" in a blue hole. Careful study of the channel was necessary before Calypso *could safely reach the big blue hole of British Honduras.*

On the 13th, she steers a course for Belize, in British Honduras.

Off the coast of Belize, in the heart of the shallow flat-top Lighthouse Reef, lies the most spectacular "blue hole" in the world. It is a legendary deep circular hole, reputed to be "bottomless" with perpendicular walls, and Captain Cousteau wishes to explore it. But it is obvious that after her accident in the Galápagos Calypso cannot continue to navigate without a thorough inspection of her hull. She leaves for the Todd Shipyards in New Orleans where the ship is dry-docked. Her false nose is rebuilt, the keel is repaired, and she is repainted. She is floated again on April 29th, and heads back to Belize.

Sounding Bottomless "Blue Holes"

Captain Cousteau arrives on May 19th; a launch, two Zodiacs and all the divers search out and laboriously mark out with dozens of buoys the two mile long, narrow, and very shallow winding channel leading to the center of the reef. In beautiful weather the ship cautiously sets out to the "hole."

She scrapes bottom only once, luckily at a sandy spot, and there is no damage. Once within the "blue hole," she makes fast with six nylon lines attached to the coral heads on the edges. From a helicopter hired for the occasion, Calypso looks like a spider at the center of its web. Diving begins. A grotto is discovered 148 feet down, where enormous stalactites hang from the ceiling. They are proof that the cave was once above sea level and that fresh water then ran over the limestone reef. Thus the level of the sea must have risen considerably. The team succeeds in bringing one of the heavy stalactites to the surface and hoisting it aboard Calypso. It will later be studied and dated as 12,000 years old by several scientific institutes, yielding valuable information on the history of the earth in this area.

The minisubs explore the "hole" all the way to the bottom, where a cone of fallen debris extends at the depth of 426 feet. Another former level of the sea is etched in the cliffs at 361 feet.

Her mission accomplished, Calypso makes for the Bahamas for a thorough study of other "blue holes," found very frequently in these islands.

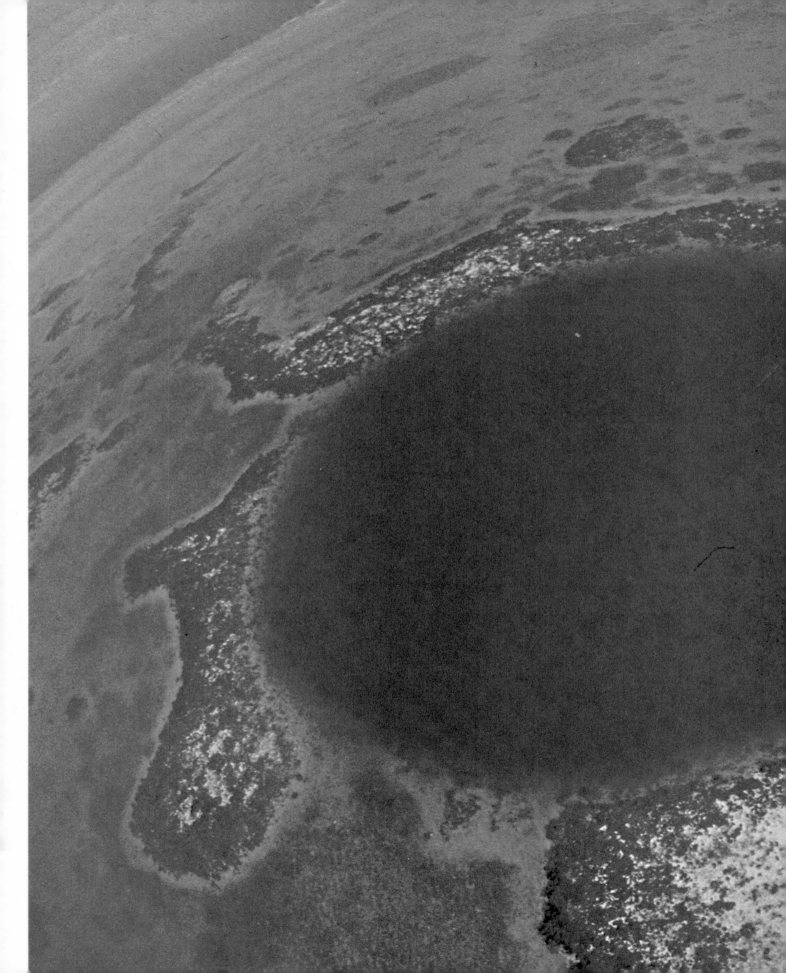

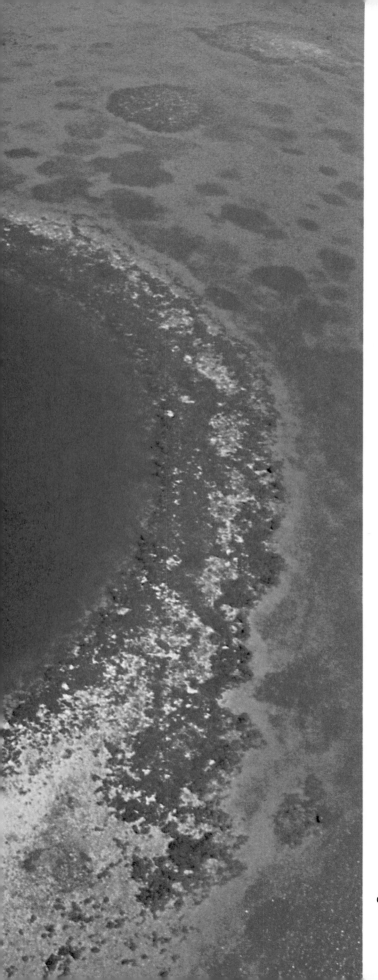

Magic of Underwater Caves

From July 11th to August 22d, a period of a month and a half, *Calypso* explores many of the 700 islands of the archipelago. The person most knowledgeable about this fantastic world, Dr. Benjamin, helps Captain Cousteau and the team search out the most interesting underwater grottos. Holes and corridors—with huge stalactites sometimes hanging from their arches—are examined and filmed without incident. However, such speleology is dangerous work, for violent tidal currents sweep through the corridors and may trap the divers.

The return trip starts from Miami; fresh food, water, and fuel are supplied in St. George in the Bermuda Islands on August 25th and in San Miguel in the Azores on September 3d.

As *Calypso* departs, the mechanics are indeed surprised to find at six o'clock in the morning that the port engine is overheating and the stern is vibrating. The engines are stopped. Michel Laval dives beneath the ship and finds a net caught in the propeller. He frees it and *Calypso* continues on her course. She passes Gibraltar on the morning of the 9th.

On September 15th, she reaches Monaco, concluding a journey of more than 50,000 miles.

Commandant Cousteau and Geologist Bob Dill watch the men bring up a stalactite weighing over a ton, found in the blue hole.

Calypso *moored in the middle of the blue hole.*

Diving saucer, minisubs, troikas, and boomers are taken along for "Operation Tunicile."

1970

Another Gas Story

Operation Tunicile

Back in Marseille, *Calypso* reports to dry dock. She is out again on the 29th of September and is commissioned to carry out an important topographical program off the coast of Sicily for a group of Tunisian and Italian industries. The study is called "Operation Tunicile" and consists of gathering a file of information in order to select the best route and best techniques for laying underwater pipelines to supply Sicily and Italy with natural gas from Algeria and Tunisia.

Calypso, commanded by Alain Thibaudeau, takes aboard the diving saucer, a minisub and two troikas. She sets out from Marseille on October 3d, in such abominable seas and winds that she is forced to take refuge in Toulon. On the 5th, *Calypso* heads for the Strait of Bonifacio. She follows the Sardinian coast and arrives in Trapani, Sicily, on the 7th, where she has a rendezvous with the two ships who are to accompany her on her expedition.

One of the pictures taken by the diving saucer on the bottom of the Strait of Messina, where currents are extremely strong.

The team begins the survey on October 8th. Echo soundings from Tunisia to Sicily are plotted. Photographic profiles are obtained by towing the troikas over the bottom. The irregularities revealed in the photographs are then inspected by the diving saucer.

Working conditions are often difficult, for *Calypso* must follow a very precise route in a heavily traveled area. Passing ships make little effort to deviate from their courses for a hydrological ship despite her distinctive signals and even though she has the right of way.

Bad seas and wretched weather in the Strait of Sicily, off Marsala, Favigrana Island, Talbot Bank, and Cape Bon, do not prevent *Calypso* from making thirty contour maps; soundings are completed by the six-hundred photographs taken during each troika haul. She also carries out twenty-eight dives in the diving saucer; five dives in the minisub; corings, dredgings, as well as current measurements and seismic profiles are made by the geophysical team from the Oceanographic Museum in Monaco. Moreover, right in the middle of the Sicilian channel, Albert Falco, while piloting the saucer on a topographical inspection, discovers the hulk of an ancient warship, almost intact and probably Phoenician, at 820 feet!

Then, from November 3d to the 7th, *Calypso* is in the Strait of Messina for six dives with the saucer. Besides very bad weather, she has to contend with currents reaching a velocity of six knots, often requiring some very acrobatic maneuvers. Flashes are broken and lost, troikas demolished, and a chain from the aliscaph *Pizzarelli* gets caught in a propeller and one of *Calypso*'s rudders. This untoward accident causes a great deal of extra work, but the project is nonetheless accomplished as planned.

On November 27th, *Calypso* is back in Marseille.

During the shooting of a film on coral fishermen in Corsica, Commandant Cousteau talks with Recco while Omer, Coll, Dr. François Laban, and Falco are gathered nearby.

1971

Dolphins and Coral Fishermen

Getting to Know Dolphins Better

A number of short scientific expeditions occupy *Calypso* for the winter months, and in March she begins a major experiment with dolphins. Dolphins are confined in an enclosure made of nets and floating in the open sea, where they are recorded, and then set free. Other experiments are made with a radio transmitter and an underwater camera attached to the back of a dolphin. Jacques Renior supervises the photography, to be finished later in Mauritania.

This program is followed by a series of seismology studies.

Red Gold

On July 6th, Captain Sirot is replaced by Captain Alain Bougaran, and *Calypso* leaves again to shoot a film on the precious red coral of the Mediterranean. For one month, Albert Falco and the film crew witness the dangerous exploits of

During the capture of dolphins near Malaga, a floating basin is set next to the hull of Calypso.

Captain Bougaran and Falco in the bridge during "Operation Dolphins."

the professional divers who use conventional air tanks down to 330 feet to gather the coral in deep caves. The price paid for coral by jewelers has created greed and caused many fatal accidents. The film is shot in Corsica, off the coast of Propriano, and in the Strait of Bonifacio. The main character is Toussaint Recco, renowned for his experience and audacity. The Galeazzi chamber and a helium breathing mixture are often used to ensure the safety of *Calypso*'s divers.

Captain Cousteau and his main associates are then monopolized by unforseen administrative problems and *Calypso* remains inactive for several months. However, the time is put to good use preparing for the most difficult, dangerous and exciting expedition in the team's entire history!

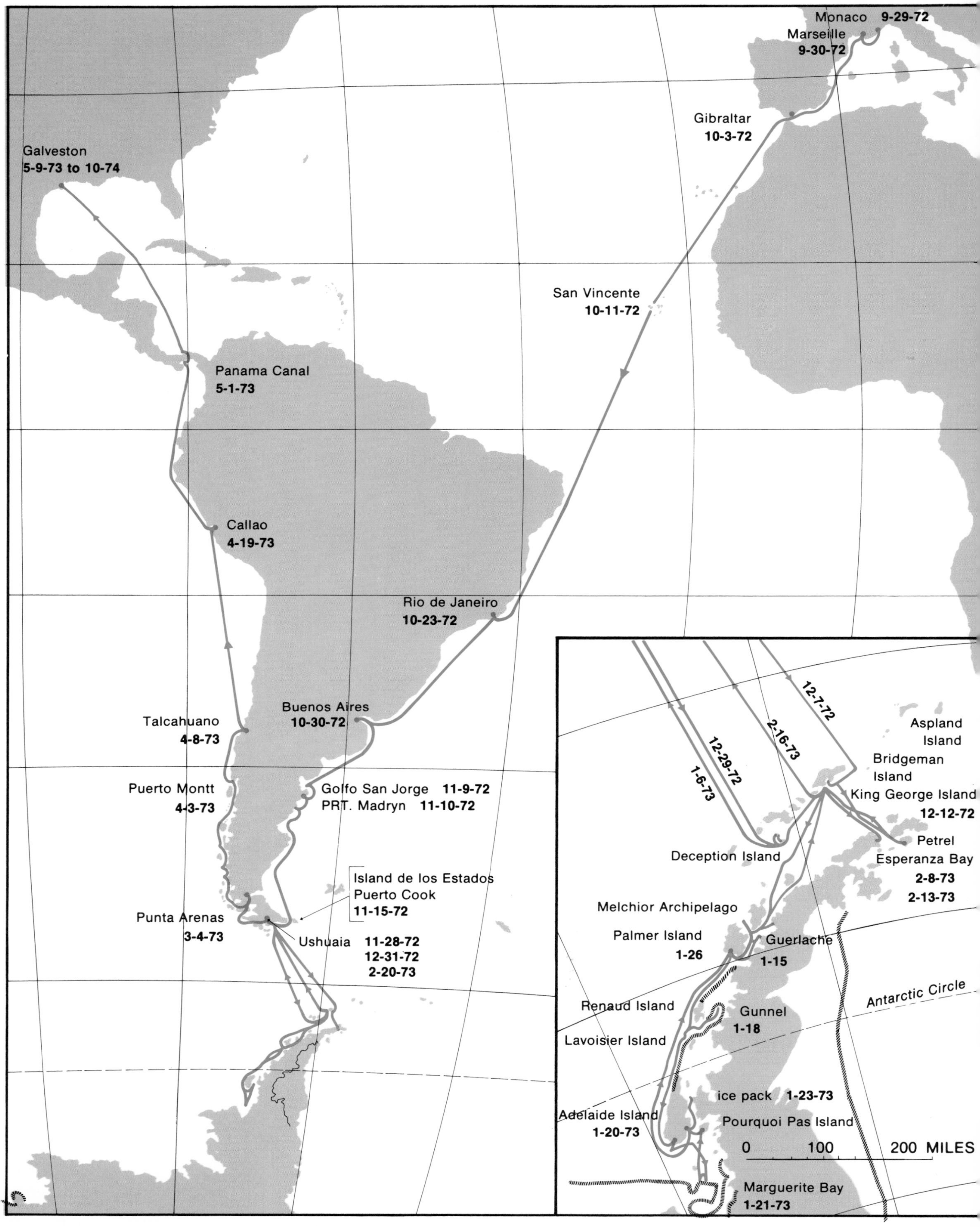

Monaco 9-29-72
Marseille 9-30-72
Gibraltar 10-3-72
Galveston 5-9-73 to 10-74
San Vincente 10-11-72
Panama Canal 5-1-73
Callao 4-19-73
Rio de Janeiro 10-23-72
Buenos Aires 10-30-72
Talcahuano 4-8-73
Puerto Montt 4-3-73
Golfo San Jorge 11-9-72
PRT. Madryn 11-10-72
Island de los Estados
Puerto Cook
11-15-72
Punta Arenas 3-4-73
Ushuaia 11-28-72
12-31-72
2-20-73
12-7-72
2-16-73
12-29-72
1-6-73
Aspland Island
Bridgeman Island
King George Island 12-12-72
Petrel
Esperanza Bay 2-8-73
2-13-73
Deception Island
Melchior Archipelago
Palmer Island 1-26
Guerlache 1-15
Renaud Island
Gunnel 1-18
Antarctic Circle
Lavoisier Island
ice pack 1-23-73
Adelaide Island 1-20-73
Pourquoi Pas Island
0 100 200 MILES
Marguerite Bay 1-21-73

Calypso ties to the ice pack and waits for the return of a group of men who went on a mission.

Amid the Ice of Antarctica

Although *Calypso* had been as far as Alaska, she had never ventured into the polar regions. After a good many discussions with friends, Captain Cousteau decides to organize a large expedition to Antarctica to explore for the first time in history the ocean depths at the edges of the icy continent with divers and with the saucer. Although sturdy, *Calypso* is obviously small and not built to withstand the assault of the ice. But she is the only ship Captain Cousteau has at his disposal.

Major repairs and many modifications are made on board ship. On September 29, 1972, before leaving Monaco, *Calypso* holds a reception aboard ship, for the many friends who wish to extend to her their best wishes for success. His Serene Highness the Prince of Monaco is present with his son Prince Albert.

Calypso puts out from Monaco loaded to capacity with equipment. The helicopter pad on the bow changes her shape a bit, but it is taken down three days later and its components stowed on the bow deck for fear it might prove dangerous in rough seas.

The weather is already bad. *Calypso* calls at Gibraltar for a day to repair a radar failure. The sea is wild. A Force 9 wind is blowing in the strait. Captain Bougaran decides to extend the stay for a few hours.

Space-Age Equipment

Calypso leaves Gibraltar on October 14th. Accompanied by many dolphins who "play" in front of the prow, she heads towards Puerto Grande,

Dwarfed by the icebergs, Calypso *searches for a sheltered area to let the saucer dive.*

Michel Laval and Commandant Cousteau collect fossils on Deception Island.

In front of a cliff of ice, the diving saucer is going to be put into the sea.

From different points on the ship, men watch, hoping to find a safe way across the ice.

in San Vicente, part of the Cape Verde Islands. On the 23d, she arrives in Rio de Janeiro, and by the 30th she is in Buenos Aires. A team from NASA installs a receiver for direct reception of photographs, in either visible or infrared light, from various satellites as they pass overhead; as well as a system of radio communication and direct image transmission, using as a relay the stationary telecommunication satellite ATS 3. *Calypso* is the first ship ever to be supplied with such equipment.

Calypso picks up a camera team led by Philippe Cousteau that had been sent in advance to Golfo San Jose and Golfo Nuevo to film right whales during their mating season.

At Port Madryn, *Calypso* embarks a Hughes 300 helicopter small enough to be kept in her hold, and capable of remaining airborne for five hours. The helicopter is to prove itself so valuable that *Calypso* will never again work without its help. On November 28th *Calypso* arrives in Ushuaia, south of Tierra del Fuego and the southernmost town in the world.

The *Bahia Aguirre*, an Argentinian ship which will be *Calypso*'s supply vessel throughout her Antarctic expedition, is docked in the port of Ushuaia. She will bring *Calypso* fuel, gasoline, kerosene, water, food, and even the saucer, which will be put in her hold so that it will not be on the quarterdeck during the crossing of Drake Passage between treacherous Cape Horn and the southern lands.

On December 5th, with snow falling, *Calypso* sails for the Shetland Islands. The weather maps transmitted by satellite and received several times a day aboard ship indicate that the timing is appropriate.

Penguins by the Millions

After a rough four-day crossing, the ship reaches St. George Island, where the helicopter and pad are quickly put up. In the meantime, the camera team and divers reconstruct the entire skeleton of a large blue whale. The bones are sorted out from the remains of thousands of whales who were flensed on the island before the huge whaling factory ships were introduced.

At Deception Island on December 19th, the cameramen find many subjects to film: seals on the beaches, and enormous rookeries of three breeds of penguins—hundreds of thousands of birds in

Shadow effect on an iceberg, courtesy of the midnight sun.

Puerto Cook, on the Island de Los Estados—the helicopter, lifted from the hold, takes off from the quarterdeck to land on the bowdeck.

the process of building their nests. The volcano still smokes through the ice and from the caldera, an immense volcanic crater, clouds of steam arise from hot-water springs.

Life in Antarctica becomes organized. The saucer makes five dives into the caldera. The divers, who are equipped with completely waterproof suits, are pleased to find that they can remain in the icy water thirty to forty minutes without undue suffering. Christmas passes. Then fate knocks at the door.

Tragedy

On December 28th, at 11:30 A.M., *Calypso*'s first mate, Michel Laval, is on Deception Island for a study of the ice involving mountain-climbing techniques. The helicopter which shuttles between *Calypso* and the island lands on the icy ground. Laval trips or slips and is struck by the helicopter's tail propeller. He is killed instantly.

Calypso has the sad task of taking Michel Laval's body back to Ushuaia. But the program contin-

ues—eleven persons, the cameramen, their assistants; the divers, their equipment and the Zodiacs are unloaded on Deception Island at the former English base called "Whalers' Bay."

Calypso arrives in Ushuaia December 31st. Michel Laval's body is put ashore on January 1, 1973 and flown by plane to Paris, accompanied by Captain Cousteau.

After stocking up on supplies, *Calypso* sails back to Deception and the team that had been left ashore returns on board.

Beyond the Antarctic Circle

Calypso passes through the Strait of Guerlache and reaches the anchorage on the Melchior Archipelago, where the *Bahia Aguirre* supplies her with fuel and water. On the 15th, *Calypso* steers a course towards the U.S. Palmer Station on the island of Anvers and then heads further south towards Renaud and Lavoisier islands. On the 17th, the ice is building up, it is snowing and visibility is almost zero. Drifting slowly, after

Philippe Cousteau is ready to ascend in his hot-air balloon.

PROPERTY OF
MATTITUCK HIGH SCHOOL
LIBRARY

changing her course—sometimes suddenly—*Calypso* finds her way with the helicopter's help, and escapes from the ice block surrounding her. The Antarctic Circle is crossed on the 19th. An iceberg 230 feet high, shaped like the Sphinx, is explored by the divers, and on the 20th, the ship is at the English base at Adelaide Island.

On the 21st, the weather turns unusually fine and clear. *Calypso* ventures into the ice pack south of Marguerite Bay, so named by Captain Charcot in honor of this wife. The sight is breathtaking. Philippe Cousteau takes advantage of the lack of wind to ascend several times in his hot-air balloon. That evening, *Calypso* berths by an iceberg and the saucer dives to a depth of 771 feet along the cliff of ice. Exploration continues around Pourquoi Pas Island and Ryder Bay, in Laubeuf Bay. Then, after a difficult passage through the narrow Gunnel Channel separating Hansen Island from Arrowsmith Peninsula, *Calypso* berths at last in Hanusse Bay, alongside the ice barrier.

A long underwater sequence is devoted to the seals that dive beneath the ice through breathing holes and are capable of swimming under the ice floe for several miles to reach open waters.

The Blizzard

After making a U-turn, *Calypso* finds herself back at the American Palmer station on the 26th, but not without first having had to struggle against the bad weather.

The helicopter, piloted by Robert McKeegan, is indispensable. The launches and Zodiacs set the course between the ice floes.

Yelcho Bay is reached on February 1st, Doumer Island on the 2d, and Cape Monaco on the 4th. *Calypso* revisits the Strait of Guerlache (where dives in the saucer reveal completely unknown forms of life at 820 feet) and reaches Esperanza Bay, an Argentinian base at the entrance to the Weddell Sea, on the 8th. That same day, the wind rises and a storm of unusual intensity sweeps across the bay, forcing the ship to veer about on her anchor with engines running to hold her against the wind and avoid, as much as possible, the huge ice floes filing past the hull. Nevertheless, one of the masses strikes *Calypso* on the stern and rips the planks, fortunately above the waterline, and also hits the port propeller, breaking its shaft.

On the 10th, it is snowing and the blizzard is raging at 100 mph. The ship is covered in a

February 10, 1973—the blizzard, raging at 100 mph, covers the ship with a shell of ice.

veritable shell of ice that weighs her down to the point of endangering her stability. On a single twisted propeller, in zero visibility, entirely dependent on radar, *Calypso* maneuvers for three days and three nights to escape disaster.

At last the wind dies down on the 11th. After dropping anchor, the crew clears the ship of her carapace of ice. The damages are repaired—after a fashion—and a survey is made to find the best way of getting *Calypso* out of the bay.

The expedition is almost finished, but *Calypso* is in bad shape. All the equipment is stowed, the saucer is lowered in the hold, and the helicopter rejoins the *San Martin*, an Argentinian icebreaker that will return to Ushuaia ahead of *Calypso*. American and Chilean sailors propose to Captain Cousteau that they take *Calypso* in tow. But this is not the first time the ship has been ill-fated and she must be able to get out of her difficulties alone. Besides, does she not have NASA equipment for picking up weather forecasts?

A shaft is broken. Divers secure the propeller so it will not jam the rudder.

From the bridge, Cousteau and Brenot watch the helicopter on the pad on the bow.

Calypso arrives in St. George Island on the 14th to await a propitious moment for the crossing of the dreaded Drake Passage.

On the 16th, the NASA weather information is better. *Calypso* sails for Ushuaia at a speed of six knots, on one engine turning at 790 revolutions. She is accompanied by the *Yelcho*, a Chilean naval vessel.

Cape Horn is in sight on the 19th.

On the 20th, the ship is safe in Ushuaia. It is a tremendous relief to everyone—not only to the team, but to all those in France, Argentina, Chile, and the United States who were anxious about *Calypso*'s fate during her difficulties.

This cruise, which had its dramatic moments, resulted in four films for television and one full-length film. Together they reveal the hitherto unknown special beauty of the marine life in Antarctica.

Tierra del Fuego— the Vanishing Patagonians

From Ushuaia, the ship sails through the Strait of Magellan and docks in Punta Arenas, a Chilean port and naval arsenal where the broken shaft is replaced, the propellers repaired, and the hole in the hull patched up.

During this period, the team takes on a new project—a study of land and marine life in the Patagonia Channels and of the life style of the last members of Indian tribes that once thrived in these underprivileged regions.

The ship is floated on the 8th and resumes her research in the channels, filming the tragic life of the 27 remaining survivors of the Kawashkar tribe, the last nomads of the sea. She returns to Punta Arenas on the 13th and travels up the Strait of Magellan to reach the coast of the Pacific Ocean once more. Ten members of the team and Captain Cousteau disembark at Puerto Montt. The saucer is sent back to France by freighter. The helicopter is put into the hold and *Calypso* sets out with a smaller crew for the port selected for her winter careening—Galveston, Texas—where she arrives on May 9, 1973. On March 4th, 1974, *Calypso*'s chief engineer, Jean-Marie France, arrives in Texas. He has the difficult task of overhauling *Calypso*, for she has indeed suffered from her Antarctic journey and from nearly a year's neglect.

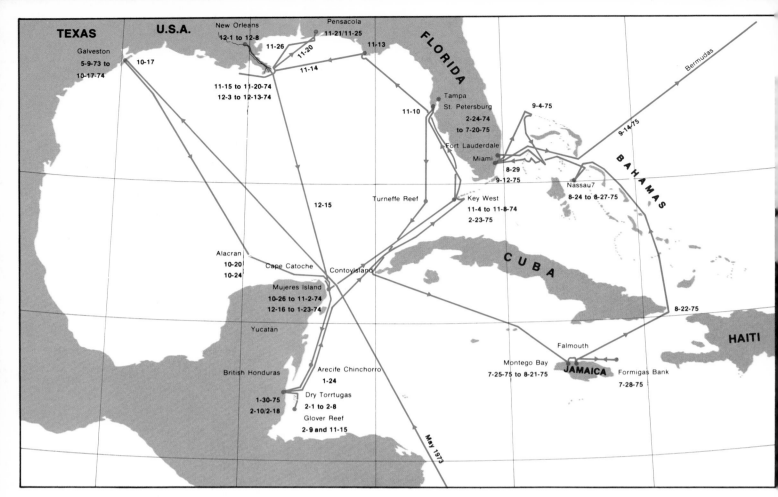

TEXAS **U.S.A.**

Galveston
5-9-73 to
10-17-74

10-17

New Orleans
12-1 to 12-8

Pensacola
11-21/11-25

11-26   11-20

11-14

11-15 to 11-20-74
12-3 to 12-13-74

FLORIDA

11-13

Bermudas

Tampa
St. Petersburg
2-24-74
to 7-20-75

9-4-75

9-14-75

11-10

Fort Lauderdale
Miami

8-29
9-12-75

Nassau7
8-24 to 8-27-75

BAHAMAS

12-15

Turneffe Reef

Key West
11-4 to 11-8-74
2-23-75

C U B A

8-22-75

Alacran
10-20
10-24

Cape Catoche

Contoy Island

Mujeres Island
10-26 to 11-2-74
12-16 to 1-23-74

HAITI

Yucatán

Falmouth

Montego Bay
7-25-75 to 8-21-75

JAMAICA

Formigas Bank
7-28-75

British Honduras

Arecife Chinchorro
1-24

Dry Torrtugas
2-1 to 2-8

Glover Reef
2-9 and 11-15

1-30-75
2-10/2-18

May 1973

1973–1974

Caribbean Surprises

Philippe Cousteau's PBY Catalina seaplane.

Calypso enters the Todd Naval Shipyards in Galveston in July and leaves in September.

A new program is in preparation. It will take place in the Caribbean and the Gulf of Mexico. Henceforth *Calypso* is to be supplemented by an amphibian plane—a PBY Catalina, specially outfitted for diving, already at work in Nicaragua, to be piloted by Philippe Cousteau.

Calypso sails on October 17th for Mujeres Island, on the northeastern tip of the Yucatán Peninsula. She soon has a breakdown because of some negligence at the shipyards, causing a three-day stop at the Alacrán Reef, 80 miles north of the coast. While repairs are being made, the team inspects the many shipwrecks that litter the windward edge of the reefs.

On the 23d, *Calypso* sails for Mujeres Island, reached on the 26th.

Off Mujeres, the observation and study of sleeping sharks takes place, eventually leading to a film. The team makes a systematic study of hydrological conditions in the caves, at 82 feet, where ocean-dwelling sharks (bull sharks and lemon sharks) take refuge and appear to sleep. This is indeed surprising, for it had long been thought that sharks had to swim continuously to keep their gills oxygenated.

The "Plume" of the Mississippi

On November 2d, *Calypso* sails for Key West, in southern Florida. She boards a team of scientists from NASA who, with their colleagues from Texas A and M University in Galveston, are to carry out a control at sea level of "remote sensing," long-distance measurements taken by planes and satellites of the chlorophyll content of the ocean. This program takes *Calypso* along the west coast of Florida, then to the mouth of the Mississippi, among the offshore oil-drilling derricks and platforms. She steers a zigzag course in the region studying the extent of the marine area polluted by the Mississippi (the Mississippi "plume") before calling at Pensacola, on November 21st.

During this period, the helicopter falls overboard and is put out of commission, but fortunately there are no injuries to the crew. It is replaced in Pensacola.

The project is resumed on November 26th. New oceanographic stations off the coast of the Mississippi Delta are made under the direction of François Varlet. The ship changes anchorages four or five times a day with several stops in between.

The survey is interrupted on December 1st, for a few days, when *Calypso* travels about a hundred miles up the Mississippi to New Orleans. After a few days in the Todd Shipyards, she resumes work.

The Long March of the Spiny Lobsters

On the 13th, *Calypso* leaves American waters to return to the Yucatán and Mujeres Island. This time the task is to study an astonishing phenomenon—the recently discovered migration of

On Mujeres Island, Paul Zuena holds one of the magnificent spiny lobsters for which Calypso *waited in vain.*

Calypso *comes across thousands of spiny lobsters caught by local fishermen in a murky sea impenetrable by the eye of the camera.*

In Galveston, Calypso *pulls away from* Texas Clipper *to head for the Todd Naval Shipyards and then the Caribbean. The French ship looks tiny next to the oceanographic vessel of Texas University.*

hundreds of thousands of tropical spiny lobsters that generally occurs at Christmastime.

On December 19th, *Calypso* is back at Mujeres. A plan is established with an extraordinary Mexican fisherman and diver, nicknamed Valvula, who had pointed out to the captain that these unusual migrations occur just after a violent northern windstorm.

The ship is near Contoy Island, north of Mujeres Island. The search and the waiting begin. A team is disembarked to pitch camp ashore, while *Calypso* sends divers down several times a day in search of the passages. Alas! Nothing turns up. Calypso travels north as far as Cape Catoche where groups of spiny lobsters are found, seeming to be waiting in their caverns for some mysterious signal to depart. On January 3d, the camp is abandoned because the wind is blowing from the wrong direction, the waters are turbid, and nothing can be examined or filmed.

On the 9th, the wind is blowing at 30 knots. *Calypso* is dragging on her anchors—she must leave, but a team returns to shore. *Calypso* shuttles back as soon as the wind abates, but too late! *Calypso* comes across some fishermen in boats

overflowing with spiny lobsters! The creatures had passed the divers' watch by the thousands in a murky sea impenetrable by the eye of the camera. *Calypso* has lost more than a month's time in a vain wait! But her camera crew, operating from the PBY seaplane, will take its revenge the following year, filming a similar migration in the Bahamas.

On the 24th, before leaving Mujeres, the team films a huge shoal of fish so close together that the helicopter takes them for an oil slick.

Group Mating of the Groupers

Calypso calls at Belize in former British Honduras on the 28th of January, explores the Glover Reef and then spends two weeks at the edge of the reefs south of Belize where thousands of groupers gather each year to spawn in a fabulous mating orgy. During that time, the local fishermen take advantage of the windfall to send out dugouts and outboards, catching on hooks and lines hundreds of large, live catches that are put into bamboo fishponds to be retrieved and killed for sale gradually as needed.

At Turneffe Reef, magnificent coral landscapes with their giant sponges are filmed day and night in 130 feet of depth.

On the 18th, it is decided to return to a familiar port—St. Petersburg, on the western coast of Florida, in Tampa Bay, for a well-earned four months of rest.

The new commander, Jean-Pierre Le Flohic, a captain in the merchant marine, is put at the disposal of French Oceanographic Expeditions by the *Messageries maritimes*.

On the 20th of July, after the usual overhaul, Captain Pierre Le Flohic takes command of *Calypso*. A new helicopter is loaded. The ship sails for Jamaica. She arrives in Montego Bay on the 24th. From this port, *Calypso* conducts an exhaustive study of the magnificent coral reefs on the northern coast of Jamaica. Maps indicate the presence of a sunken ship near the Formigas Shoal, 100 miles to the east. Piloted by Bob Braunbech, the helicopter flies to the area and finds the ship easily, owing to the extraordinary clarity of the water, and guides the divers to the wreck by radio.

Working closely with biologists from the marine biology station at Discovery Bay, Philip Dustan and *Calypso*'s divers explore and film the coral cliffs which extend from 30 to 650, sometimes even 1,000 feet below the surface. The phenomenon of "cannibalism" among certain species of coral is filmed with the aid of a time-lapse photographic device improvised aboard ship. Flower-shaped coral formations 12 to 20 feet in diameter found at depths of 100 to 200 feet are filmed, as are deeper colonies of coral living at 240 feet or more.

Sea Charts Drawn by Satellite?

After skirting Cuba, *Calypso* arrives in Nassau on August 24th, where a new series of pioneering experiments is started in collaboration with NASA. The idea is to use satellites LANSAT 1 and LANSAT 2 to verify and/or to update marine maps in the shallow areas of the sea, those that condition the safety of navigation. The Bahamas are chosen as the experimental area.

From August 25th to September 8th, while the satellites photograph three well-defined areas of the huge Bahamian reefs, *Calypso* spends her time mapping the bottom, measuring water transparency and the reflective properties of diverse marine sediments and coral bottoms. The work is carried out with sonar, helicopter, and divers handling various instruments. The results, analyzed in 1976, show that satellites can indeed be used for keeping sea charts up to date to a depth of almost 100 feet.

On September 8th, *Calypso* returns to Miami. It is the end of the expedition. After a few repairs, *Calypso* sets out on her way home. It is her eighth Atlantic crossing. An American deck officer, Lieutenant Lockart, who already was on board in 1974, will complete the crew. On the morning of October 7th, *Calypso* reaches Marseille and is overhauled without delay.

On October 24th, once more as good as new, *Calypso* returns to Monaco where her next project is to be hatched.

In Jamaica, a new pad for the helicopter is set abaft.

Cousteau, Giacoletto, and Falco on Psira Island.

A Remembrance of Things Past

In the autumn of 1975, *Calypso* is about to leave on a long underwater archaeology program. The team will search the Aegean Sea for new traces of vanished civilizations—submerged cities, harbors, and shipwrecks from all ages. The funds required for the expedition are almost all provided by film contracts and by a nonprofit American foundation called the Cousteau Society. The operation of *Calypso*, of the PBY, and of the diving saucer is, from then on, entirely entrusted to the Cousteau Society.

On October 30th, at eleven o'clock, Captain Cousteau holds a press conference in *Calypso*'s mess— a room too small to hold the entire audience. At the conference's end, one of the journalists is heard to say as he leaves: "We learn more with

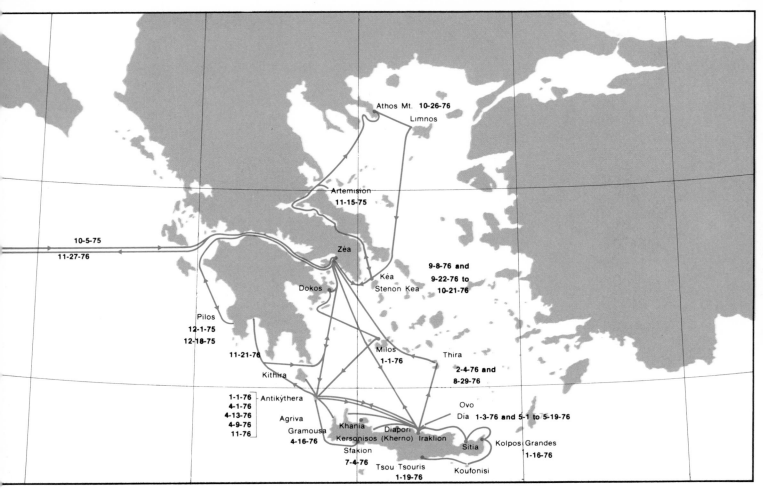

1975–1976

Cousteau in an hour and a half then we do with all the others in years!"

The next day, *Calypso* leaves Monaco under Captain Pierre Mahé. She follows the west coast of Corsica, the Strait of Bonifacio, the Strait of Messina, passes through the Canal of Corinth, and arrives at Marina Zéa, near Pireus, on the evening of November 4th.

A Quest for Sunken Ships

Calypso receives directly from the United States a new "side-scan" sonar together with its electric winch. Developed by Harold Edgerton, who will be aboard to operate it for two months, this device enables *Calypso* to detect objects lying on the bottom of the sea within a range of 500 yards on each side of the ship's course. Harold has been a regular "Calypsonian" for 20 years.

Calypso is thus well equipped to find remains of sunken ships. . . . But the sea is immense. Discovery in undersea archaeology is a matter partly of logic, but mostly of patient research—making inquiries among the native fishermen and rummaging through history archives for accounts of battles, shipwrecks, and natural catastrophes. *Calypso*'s helicopter permits easy communication between the islands, the ship, and the neighboring ports.

The first sorties are made off the coast of Zéa, then to the southeast near Patroklou, off the coast of Cape Sounion, and near Kéa Island. After systematic plotting between November 11th and the 15th, a large sunken ship is located 62 fathoms deep. It is the wreck of the *Britannic,* the sister ship of the *Titanic.* Serving as a hospital ship during World War I, the largest vessel afloat at her time was sunk in mysterious circumstances in 1916.

131

Venerable Remains

Calypso spends one month looking almost in vain for the remains of the vessel that must have transported the magnificent bronze statues of Poseidon, of a horse and of a jockey, found at the turn of the century near Cape Artemísion. Only pottery and a bronze vase are recovered. Then a thorough investigation of the Bay of Pílos, where the famous battle of Navarino took place, is made during the following month. All the remaining bits and parts still sticking out of the mud are plotted by side-scan sonar and visited by divers.

After a general exploration of the reef and islands

Fishermen come to see the ship, anchored at Día Island.

of the central Aegean, *Calypso* calls at Heraklion, in Crete, and starts a thorough investigation of the island of Día. Four ancient shipwrecks are located, as well as many huge Venetian anchors. Just when *Calypso* was about to leave, an important archaeological discovery is made: Falco identifies, in the bay of St. George, an antique, submerged harbor! Special equipment will be necessary to excavate the site. While exploring the eastern part of Crete, another important discovery is made: a wall of Minoan pottery, close to the islet of Pina, down 100 feet.

From February 6th to March 3d, *Calypso* stays in port at Marina Zéa, allowing part of the crew to return to France and some maintenance work to be done.

A Flood of Artifacts for the Museum

On March 24th, Captain Yves Gourlawen takes command of the ship. An improvised pontoon, an air compressor, and an underwater air lift are installed in the bay of St. George in Día at the site of the contemplated excavation of the antique harbor.

Calypso makes numerous shuttles between Heraklion and Día. Hundreds of amphorae, pottery, copper and silver plates, marbles, and wood from the hulls of four ships are salvaged, after careful photography and mapping.

From April 13th to April 20th, a foray is made to the famous sunken ship at Antikýthēra. The site is difficult to identify, and is carefully photographed. A photo mosaic of the bottom is carefully assembled by Captain Cousteau.

Día still occupies most of *Calypso*'s time between April 23d to May 20th. After two months of efforts, the team on shore completes an underwater systematic excavation of an area measuring 10 yards by 10 yards and located close to the sunken jetty of the harbor. The air lift allows us to reach the base rock, 10 feet under the mud, and the discovery in the lower layers of Minoan pottery proves that Falco's harbor was already in use in 2000 B.C.

It is impossible to mention all the artifacts brought up from the sea during this expedition. Everything was handed over to the Greek Ministry for Cultural Affairs and taken in charge by Greek museums. Among the interesting objects are a magnificent bronze cannon, pulled from the French vessel, *La Thérèse,* north of Crete, as well as hundreds of amphorae, pottery, copper plates, marble blocks, and Minoan cups, from a dozen locations. The great composer, Mikis Theodorakis, came on board twice and made a saucer dive.

Thíra (Santorin), with its impressive underwater crater, was also thoroughly explored. The explosion of Thíra in 1450 B.C. had considerable influence on the history of Mediterranean civilizations.

The Deepest Grandmother

On September 20, 1976, the most difficult dives made in Greece begin—to the sunken ship *Britannic.* A submersible Galeazzi decompression chamber, a breathing mixture of three gases (helium, nitrogen, and oxygen), large-capacity aqualungs, cables, slings, and anchors are all aboard *Calypso,* which is to serve as a diving base for almost a month, from September 23d to October 20th. St. Nikolò on Kéa Island is the nearest base to the sunken ship. *Calypso* returns there every evening to avoid the risk of nighttime collisions.

While the saucer dives, explores, and films, the SDC is submerged to a depth of 130 feet. Three divers equipped with oversized tanks filled with the helium mixture leave the ship, and descend for fifteen minutes down to 370 feet, explore the sunken ship, and then slowly ascend up to the chamber. They enter the SDC and close it off. The chamber is hoisted aboard ship and a slow decompression of 2 hours and 40 minutes takes place under the medical supervision of Doctor Pierre Caborou. No diver ever suffered any ill effects.

The goal of these difficult and costly dives was to determine:

1. If the *Britannic,* a hospital ship, had been illegally transporting war materiel as the Germans had claimed in 1916.
2. Why this huge "unsinkable" ship went down after only one blow, whether mine or torpedo.

A remarkable visitor is invited to make a saucer dive to the *Britannic:* Mrs. Macbeth Mitchell, a Scottish woman and survivor of the *Britannic* where she had been serving as a nurse. The alert and dynamic 86-year-old woman declares that the *Britannic* is now more beautiful than before, and says jokingly that she would like us to recover her alarm clock from cabin 15!

At Zéa, Calypso *takes on board a raft and a compressor, to establish a fixed site at Día Island.*

The submersible Galeazzi decompression chamber is lowered into the water to facilitate dives to the wreck of *the* Britannic.

Calypso *at berth in Monaco before heading for new missions.*

Captain Cousteau himself made two deep helium dives, in particular to the ship's holds, to examine them thoroughly. *Calypso*'s investigation concluded that the *Britannic* was not carrying any war materiel or military equipment and had indeed been sunk by a mine laid a few weeks earlier by the German submarine U73. But the explosion hit the coal bunker, setting a second explosion of the coal dust. The war crime was anonymous.

Art and Jewels 2,000 Years Old

From November 1st to the 23d, *Calypso*, with the archaelogist Lazare Kolonas, returns, for the last time, to the famous sunken ship at Antikýthēra.

The suction pipe is used extensively to dig out gold jewelry, cut-glass cups, vases, fine pottery, and above all, two magnificent bronze statuettes from the Hellenic Age (second or third century B.C.) They are all now in the National Museum in Athens.

After stopping at the dock in Piraeus, the ship enters the Channel of Corinth with a smaller crew aboard, crosses the Strait of Messina and returns to Monaco in miserable weather.

Calypso is at the dock on December 1, 1976. Our chronicle ends here, but the adventures of this plucky little ship are, without doubt, far from being over! The year 1977 is devoted to an unprecedented survey of the entire Mediterranean Sea, including the Black Sea, to measure the exact degree of pollution and to choose the most beautiful sites that deserve protection.

134

Appendix

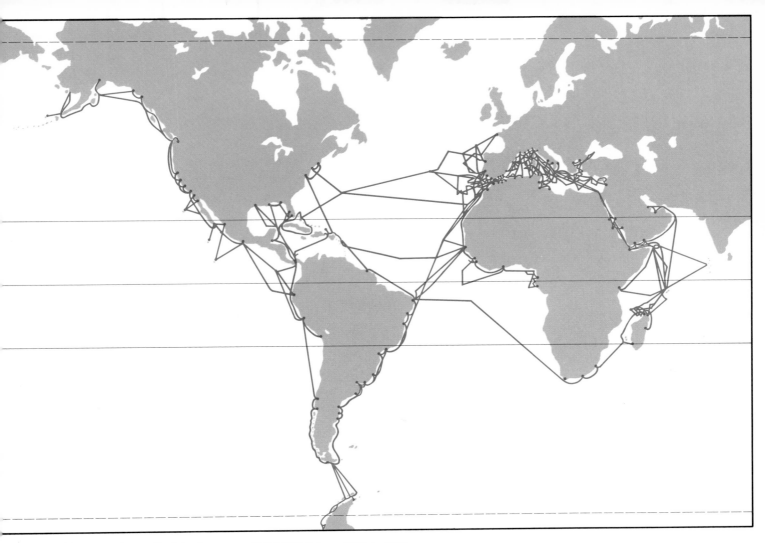

This map shows all of the journeys of CALYPSO from 1951 to 1973

History of the CALYPSO prior to her becoming an oceanographic ship

The boat, which would later bear the name *Calypso,* was built in Seattle in the state of Washington on the west coast of the United States in the Ballard Marine RLY shipyard under the provisions of the lend lease act for the Royal Navy.

Destined to be a mine sweeper, the BYMS 26, it was started May 21, 1942, and finished August 20, 1942.

It was one of a series of 561 sweepers constructed in 2 years, and of which 33 were lost by acts of war. Entirely constructed of wood, it was equipped with the latest equipment for classic, magnetic, or acoustical sweeping.

Inscribed under the number 191,018 in the Royal Navy, it had the number 2000 added to its original I.D. number, and became the No. 2026, starting in December 1943, so that it would not be confused with the American YMS series.

It's bell bore the inscription: HMS. JB26 1942, the letter J indicating that it was a minesweeper for the Royal Navy, and the letter B for the BYMS series.

Along with the BYMS 9, 19, 22, and 27, constituting the 153rd M/S Flotilla, it left Seattle the 28th of February 1943 for Gibraltar via San Francisco and Freetown.

It was in Freetown in May 1943. In August 1943, while based in Malta, the flotilla was reduced to five boats. On September 19, 1943, the BYMS 19 exploded over a mine near Cortione in Italy and sank.

The flotilla was based in Malta between 1943 and 1944, at Tarente from 1944–1945, and Naples from 1945–1946, and then was disbanded.

The JB 26 returned to the base in Malta in July 1946, and was returned to the U.S. Navy on August 1, 1947, which put it up for sale along with its other minesweepers.

It wasn't until May 1949 that a buyer presented himself in the person of Mr. Joseph Gazan, forwarding agent in Malta, who wanted to establish a local coastal service.

The boat had already been stripped of its military equipment, and Mr. Gazan had only to dismount and remove the magnetic sweeping equipment.

The hull was in very good condition, and the motors worked well; a few changes were made, and there was the JB 26, turned into a ferry boat making the run between the two principal islands of the archipelago, Malta itself and Gozo.

Its baptism was a solemn occasion, and the blessing was given by the archbishop of Malta, Msgr. Michael Gonzi. This baptism was to give the boat, which had never before been designated except by its number, a name to call its own, Calypso.

The sponsor was Mr. Gazan himself, and the reason for his choice was that the island of Gozo, which would be serviced by the boat, was, according to numerous commentators on the text of Homer, the island of Ogygia of the nymph Calypso. This was the same Calypso who, having captured the brave and wise Ulysses, held him prisoner for seven years and would not release him except on the order of Jupiter himself.

Several months later, the Calypso was sent to Sicily where the rear of the boat was in part reconstructed. After that, Calypso could make its crossings with 11 cars and 400 passengers.

One of these trips was especially memorable, for with great pomp and all the ostentation of such an event, she transported the relic of the head of Saint Anthony, amidst the enthusiasm of the faithful Maltese and profoundly Catholic inhabitants of Gozo.

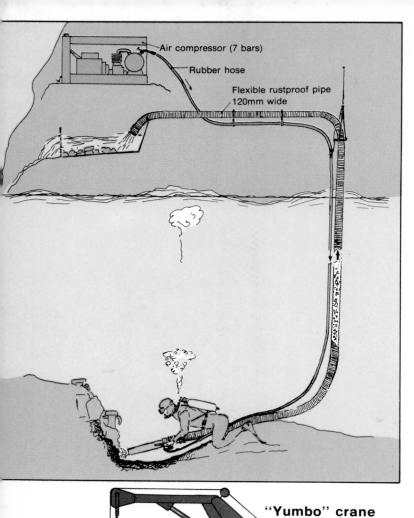

Air compressor (7 bars)

Rubber hose

Flexible rustproof pipe
120mm wide

Underwater Work (at left)

Oxygen tank in action at Grand Congloue. Air arriving at the bottom of the big tube forms an emulsion with the water which is lighter than the water and which rises easily when there is a strong suction on the mouthpiece.

Simplified Diagram of the Hydraulic Equipment of the Calypso
(below)

The crane "Yumbo" can be used either with its own central hydraulic system or with the central hydraulic system of the winches.

The Yumbo unit is a simple compressor type with a fixed flow which always turns in the same direction at a constant speed. The machine is started and controlled by the 4 distributors that are maneuvered by knobs.

The "Duclos" hydraulic unit includes a pump that always rotates in the same direction but with variable flow in both quantity and direction. The winches can be operated in either direction, up or down, by using the command wheel.

To operate the crane in an emergency, the variable-flow pump is placed in a fixed position with the flow in the proper direction.

Winches

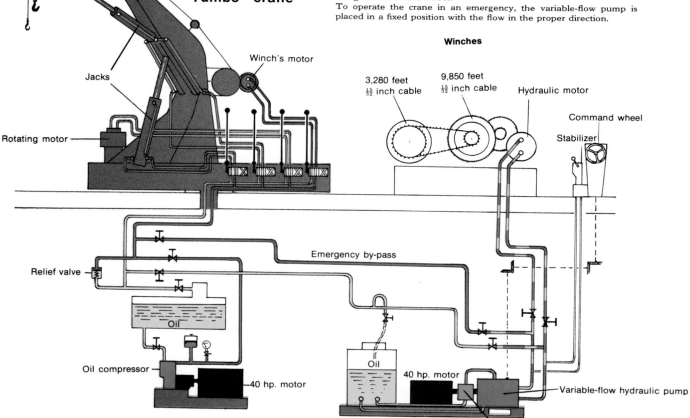

"Yumbo" crane

Winch's motor

Jacks

Rotating motor

3,280 feet
$\frac{1}{2}$ inch cable

9,850 feet
$\frac{1}{2}$ inch cable

Hydraulic motor

Command wheel

Stabilizer

Relief valve

Emergency by-pass

Oil

Oil

Oil compressor

40 hp. motor

40 hp. motor

Variable-flow hydraulic pump

Feeding pump

Yumbo-Marel Hydraulic unit
Maximum pressure: 90 bars

"Duclos" hydraulic unit
Maximum pressure: 120 bars
Used at 60 bars

138

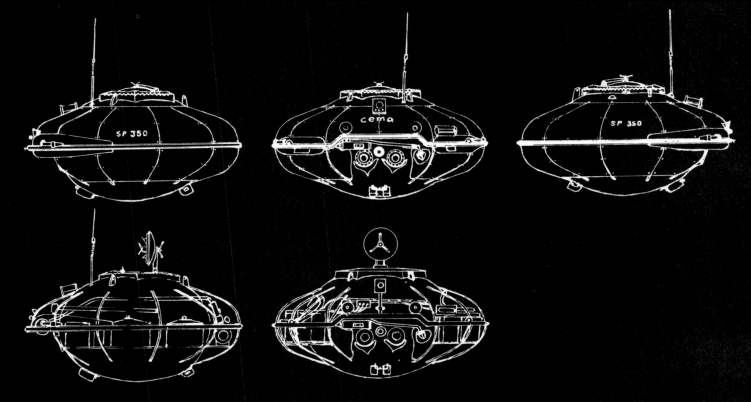

Diagram of the saucer without the hull

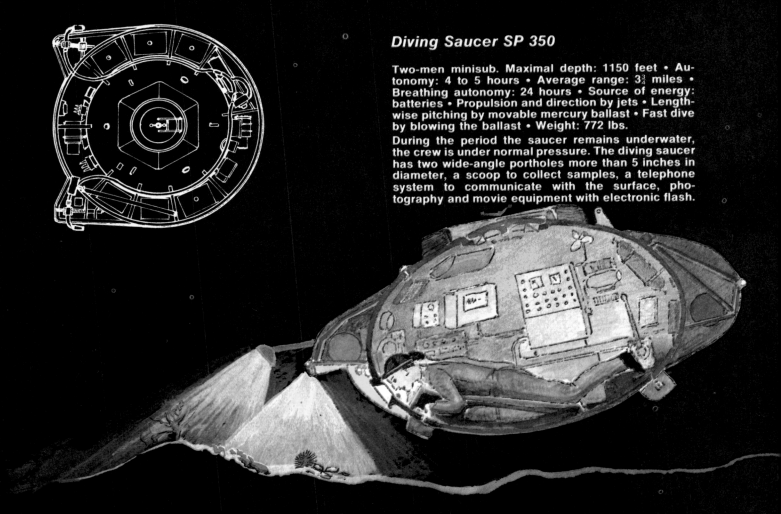

Diving Saucer SP 350

Two-men minisub. Maximal depth: 1150 feet • Autonomy: 4 to 5 hours • Average range: 3¾ miles • Breathing autonomy: 24 hours • Source of energy: batteries • Propulsion and direction by jets • Lengthwise pitching by movable mercury ballast • Fast dive by blowing the ballast • Weight: 772 lbs.

During the period the saucer remains underwater, the crew is under normal pressure. The diving saucer has two wide-angle portholes more than 5 inches in diameter, a scoop to collect samples, a telephone system to communicate with the surface, photography and movie equipment with electronic flash.

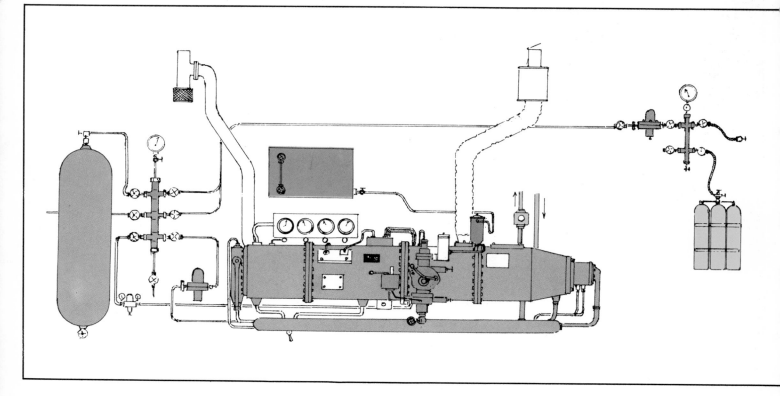

"Junker" compressors

"Junkers" compressors, made in Germany, built for submarines during the Second World War (Blow the ballasts). Type 4FK 115 — Four stages — Output 132 gph — Pressure 200 bars — Saltwater cooling system — Average power 30 hp — Used to fill the diving tanks. *Calypso* has two "Junkers" with four tanks of 132 gallons each.

Trawlers: Devices used to take pictures at great depths (Troikas) Top: Hanging type of Edgerton Camera and Flash 1954. Top right: Same device but installed on first model of trawler; 1 picture every 15 seconds. Bottom: Photography or cinematography equipment made by Prof. Edgerton, installed on a 1958 trawler called "Troika."

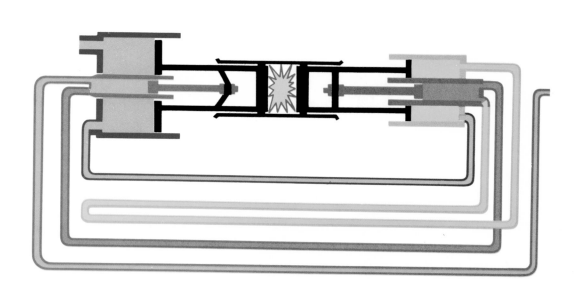

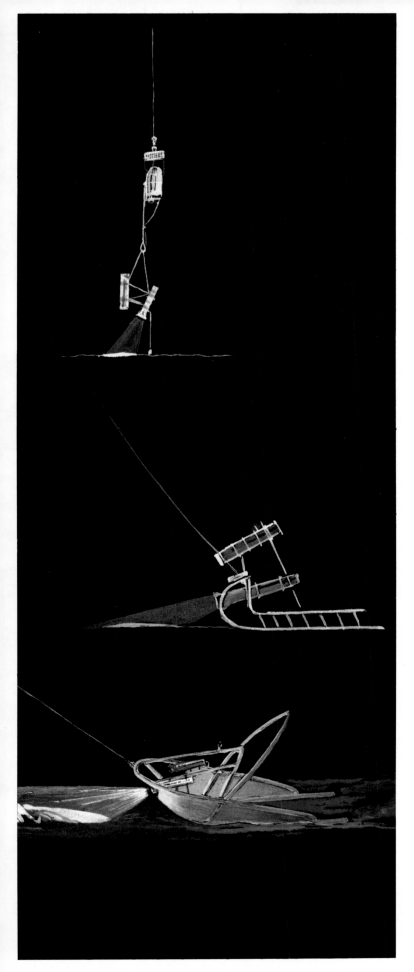

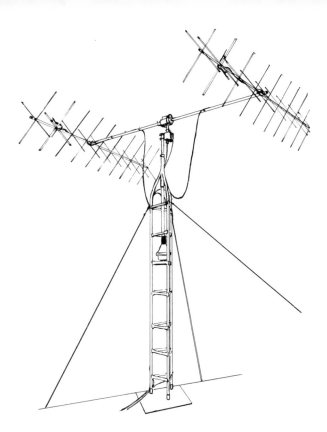

Simplified diagram showing the system of communications between Calypso, NASA, and the weather satellites.

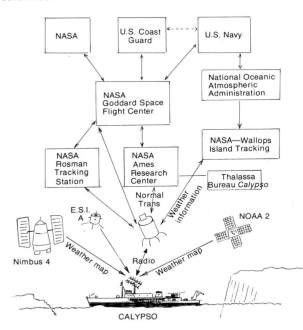

Exploration seaplane Consolidated "Catalina" — PBY, annex of *Calypso*
Wingspan 103 feet — Length 64 feet — Weight 34,030 lbs. — Engines two Pratt and Whitney "Twin Wasp" R 1830, 1,200 hp — Speed 314 mph — Range 3,800 miles — Maximum altitude almost 20,000 feet.

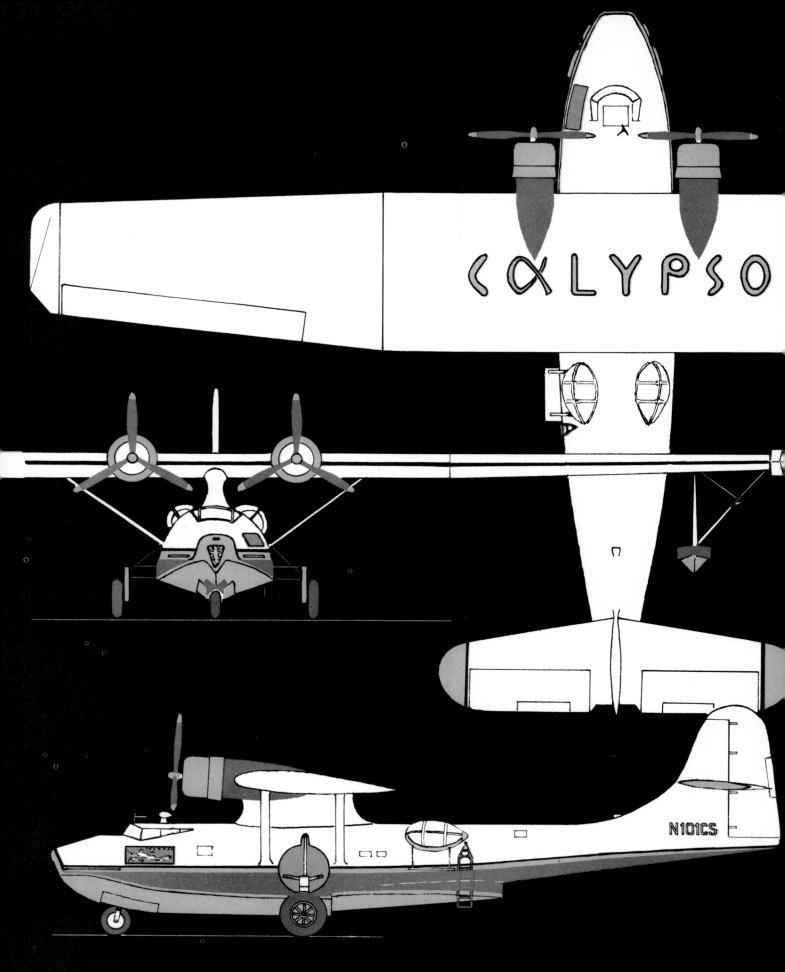

Contents

Photo credits

French Oceanographic Company · Requins Associates · C.E.M.A. · O.F.R.S. ·
Cousteau Society · Cousteau Group · Robert Pollio · Jacques Roux · Alexis Sivirine
· Paul Zuena · and various members of the Cousteau expedition

Index

PROPERTY OF
MATTITUCK HIGH SCHOOL
LIBRARY

81806

For Reference

Not to be taken from this room